# FIRE ON THE MOUNTAIN
## BOOK ONE
# THE PATH

## RICK JOYNER

MorningStar Publications

*Fire On The Mountain: The Path*
by Rick Joyner
Copyright ©2013
Fourth Printing

---

**Distributed by MorningStar Publications, Inc.,**
**a division of MorningStar Fellowship Church**
**375 Star Light Drive, Fort Mill, SC 29715**

**www.MorningStarMinistries.org**
**1-800-542-0278**

---

---

Cover Design: Eunjoo Jun
Book Layout: Kandi Evans

ISBN— 978-1-60708-524-9; 1-60708-524-0

For a free catalog of MorningStar Resources, please call 1 800 542 0278

# TABLE OF

# CONTENTS

# CHAPTER ONE

# THE VOICE

I thought every step would be my last. The hunger, thirst, and weariness all combined into the greatest crisis I had ever experienced. Death had to be very close. The fog was so thick I could only see a few feet in front of me, and it seemed to perfectly fit my mental state. I was determined not to stop as long as I was still conscious, but I knew that could not be much longer.

I was trudging through a dense forest on a narrow path. My eyes burned. My clothes were frayed so badly they hardly gave any protection from the thorns and sharp limbs that stabbed at me continually. I had gone far beyond the point where I thought I could not go any further and each step was torture. Death became desirable. Even so, if I died I did not want it to be because I gave up. I knew that if I ever stopped I would not be able to start again, so I plodded on step by tortured step.

I thought of why I had entered this wilderness. I had been shown a great purpose on the other side. Now my whole purpose was to die while still trying to go forward. This would at least be some measure of victory against this wilderness that now seemed sure to be my doom.

Just when I was sure my next step would be my last I saw a faint sparkle through the fog ahead. I thought I must have imagined it and that my mind was playing tricks on me, but I gathered all of the resolve that I had to stumble forward a few more feet. I saw it again. It could not be very far, so I determined to reach whatever it was.

I emerged from the forest and was standing in front of a small lake. It was the most beautiful water I had ever seen, not just because I was so thirsty, but it was like a scene out of heaven. The water was a deep blue that sparkled from within. Large rocks and trees seemed to have been arranged around it for a special beauty. It looked completely natural and yet divinely landscaped.

I tried to kneel down, but fell on my face at the edge of the water. As thirsty as I was I just stared at it for a long moment. The water seemed alive with light. It then occurred to me that it must be some kind of radioactive pool. It could kill me to drink it.

"So what!" I thought. "I'm going to die if I don't drink it, so I might as well try it." Still, I cautiously dipped the tip of my finger into the water and touched it to my tongue. It felt and tasted strange. It was charged with some kind of energy, but it was also sweet. I felt energy and drank more. The more I drank, the stronger I felt.

I kept drinking until I felt stronger than I ever had in my life. It was as if every cell in my body was being awakened. Just moments before I felt worse than I ever had, and now I felt better than I ever had. I went from hell to heaven, from being on the edge of death to being more alive than I had ever been. I was in awe.

I began to look around. My eyes had brightened so that I could see through the fog. The water had not only quenched my thirst, but my hunger as well. "What kind of water is this?" I thought. Then I began to think that the water had been radioactive and had done something very strange to me physically. I considered that it probably would kill me pretty soon, but it would be a wonderful way to die! I felt so good it was hard to be negative about anything.

The mental clarity was as invigorating as the energy I felt flowing through my body. I could never remember feeling this good or sharp. As I looked around I seemed to take in every detail quickly. I saw things I would have never noticed before even if I had stared for a long time. My mind was going at hyper-speed, but with order and precision.

I was thinking that if I would have had this water while going through the wilderness, it would have been the most enjoyable journey ever, not the death walk it had been. I was then startled to see a man standing so close that I could not believe I had not seen him approaching, especially with the way I was able to see and take in so much.

"Who are you?" I asked. "Does this water belong to you?"

"This water belongs to anyone who will drink it," he replied.

"Are you an angel?" I asked.

"No. I am a man like you," he replied. He stared at me for a moment and then continued, "The stream that feeds this pool was very close to you in the wilderness you just came through. You could have refreshed yourself with it at any time."

"I did not see any stream in that wilderness," I protested.

"You did not see it because you did not look for it," he replied, dispassionately.

This was a shocking thought. If I could have had this water through the wilderness I would have run through it singing praise to God instead of suffering the torture I endured!

"I was not told anything about this water in the wilderness," I replied.

"Even the youngest disciples are taught where to find this water and how to drink from it daily. Is there no discipleship left? Did you not have a mentor to teach you this?" he said.

"No. I did not have a mentor. And there is not much discipleship left," I answered.

The visitor hung his head as if deeply grieved. Finally he continued, "Well, your endurance was impressive. It will serve you well on this journey, but you must save your endurance for the battles ahead. The wilderness is intended to be hard, but not as hard as you made it. The living water is available to sojourners at any time and in any place, if you stay on the right path. When you are on the right path it will always be close to you, so find it, drink it often, and never go far from it. This is one of the most basic lessons you must learn for where you are headed and what you are called to do."

"I don't think you will have to tell me that again," I responded, "but how do you know where I'm going and what I'm called to do?"

"I've been waiting for you and the others. I'm here to help you. There have not been many coming this way in recent times. This has to be the result of there not being much discipleship left. Are there no fathers left?"

"Spiritual fathers and mothers are rare in these times," I said. "I think, in general, the leaders have given themselves to building organizations more than building people. We do have some great ministries and organizations being raised up, but great saints are becoming rare."

"What about you?" he inquired.

"I am as guilty as anyone else. I have not been a good father or mentor. I too have spent more time building organizations than building people," I replied.

"Would you do it differently if you got another chance?" the visitor asked, looking at me as if this was the most important question he could ask.

"I would like to try," I answered. "I've always been clumsy in relationships, but I know how important it is. I just have not done much about it."

"You are correct," the visitor replied. "The world has had the greatest ingathering of new believers in history in your time, but very few are are finding this path. If they do not come here they will not be prepared for what is coming upon the earth. If they are not prepared,they will be lost."

"What is coming?" I asked.

"Do you not know where you're going?"

"I do know I am going to the mountain, but you spoke of something coming. What is coming?" I asked.

"I know you have been to the mountain and that you have fought battles there, but what is coming is the greatest battle there has ever been on the earth. It is the last battle.

"We are here to prepare you for your purpose, to finish what has been lacking in your training, which is much more than I was expecting. We must get started. I've brought you these," he said, and held up a new set of clothes that he laid on a nearby branch.

I looked at the clothes and then back at him, but he was gone. I was sure he could not have moved fast enough to get beyond my vision that quickly, yet I could not see him. I thought he must have been an angel as I turned to look at the clothes.

The clothes were made out of a material so thin and light they did not seem to have any weight. I thought they would be too fragile to wear. I tried to make a small tear in the tunic to test it, but as hard as I tried I could not tear it. I then tried to poke a small hole in it with a sharp stick, but as hard as I tried I could not even make a mark on it.

I removed my torn rags, washed in the pool of water, and put on the new clothes. There were boots, a cape, and a hat, all made out of the same material, and they all fit perfectly. I then heard the voice of the man who had just been with me coming from the forest. I could not see anyone in the direction the voice seemed to be coming from.

"They are more than clothes. They are part of your armor. You will need it to get where you are going now."

"Where am I going now?" I asked.

"You are going to your home."

"Who are you?" I asked, still looking for the source of the voice. "Where is my home?"

"I am the Voice that cries in the wilderness," he said as he stepped out of the forest so close that I could not believe I had not seen him. Then he continued as if he had heard my thoughts.

"You did not see me because I cannot be seen until I move. Are you prepared for this journey?" he asked, looking at me with great intensity.

"With this living water I feel ready for anything, but honestly the answer would have to be 'no.' I am not prepared. I know I'm going to the mountain, but I don't know how to get there other than to follow this path. I have not been this way before," I replied.

"I am not surprised. Those coming here now are like an army that does not even know how to hold their weapons, much less use them. Even those who have been leaders of thousands who show up here are weak, with minds that have not been renewed or transformed. They are worldly, foolish, and not prepared even for this journey, much less for what is coming upon the earth," he lamented.

"I'm sorry. I'm as guilty as anyone, but what can we do about it?" I asked.

"We must do the best we can with what we're given to work with, but we are getting very close to the last battle. It will be the climax of the ages, the ultimate battle between light and darkness. You are so far from being ready for it," the Voice continued to lament.

"I've never known anything but battles my whole life. I've known the last battle is near, and I've been preaching and writing about it for years. But not many want to hear about it, and of those who will hear it, few will act on it. I don't even think I have done much to act on it. Few have set their affections on things above and not the things that are on the earth.

"I've not been here before," I continued, "but it does seem familiar. I do not know what you mean by 'my home.' I've had many homes. Am I going to one of them?"

"Do you remember what you were seeking when you began this journey?" he asked.

"I do," I replied.

"You are seeking the city that God is building. You want to be a part of what He is doing, not just what men are doing. That is what everyone who comes here is seeking," the Voice continued. "This seems familiar because you have been here before. You have passed this place a few times in the circles you have been going in. You will understand all of this in due time, but you are right to think that you are not ready for the journey. You are not ready."

"What do I do to get ready?" I asked.

"You are already doing the main thing—walking this path. You admitted to not understanding even the basics about the living water. You do not feel ready. Maybe you are humble enough to learn what you need fast enough. It is those who think they are ready who are always the first to get lost here."

"I really do not remember being at this pool before, but I do feel that everything is familiar," I said. "You even seem familiar."

"Everything here changes over time," the Voice continued. "You have been here before, but it did not look like this. You must understand this for the journey. The familiar things you are looking for to give you bearings are not the same, and you are not the same. Therefore, your guidance must come from your heart, your spirit. You must see with the eyes of your heart more clearly than you see with these eyes, or you will not stay on the right path."

"There is more than one path?" I asked.

"Yes, and all but one go to a place you do not want to go. There are delusions, deceptions, distractions, and traps all along the path. They are all there to divert you from your purpose. It will take more discernment, more wisdom, and more courage to stay on the right path than anyone has."

"Then how can I make it?" I asked.

"You will need help. You will need the Helper. You will have to depend on Him and stay humble enough to keep depending on Him.

"You must also have the living water. You must never let it out of your sight again. You must drink from it as soon as you begin to thirst. Even drink when you are not thirsty when you can. It will keep you alive. Staying close to it will help keep you on the path."

Everything he said seemed to go deep into my heart because my perception was so keen. I felt that I could recall everything perfectly anytime I needed to. I have been such a concept-oriented person that I struggle to remember details accurately and consider this one of my greatest weaknesses. I was elated that I could perceive and remember every detail with such clarity and depth now. I felt as if a whole new part of my mind had been opened.

The Voice drew his head back as if he was suddenly inter- ested in something and said,

"You have understanding. The mental clarity you now have is because the Spirit quickens your mortal body. The Spirit will turn your weaknesses into strengths. If you will walk in the Spirit, you will always be strong in what you need. To make it to your destiny, you must abide in the Spirit. The waters you are drinking are Spirit and life. It was the Spirit that quickened Moses so that he did not grow weaker with age, but stronger, and his eyes never grew dim."

"Do you mean I can feel like this from now on?" I asked.

"You can, and even more so. It is up to you. How well you learn this will determine how well you do on this journey and whether or not you complete it. To feel as you do now, to think as you can now, and to be able to see as you can now, is the natural state of the new creation you are."

"I don't think I have ever been as close to death as I was just a few minutes ago," I said. "After drinking this water, I don't think I have ever been this alive. I have a mental clarity I don't remember ever having except when I was before the throne. Just a few minutes ago I could hardly think at all. Now you say I can be this way all of the time?"

The Voice moved to stand right in front of me and looked intently into my eyes, and said, "You not only can, you must remain as you are now. When you are in the Spirit, you are before the throne. His kingdom is within. The King is in you. You are His temple. To walk in truth is to know this and to live in His presence.

"Until one is born again they cannot see the kingdom. But just because they are born again does not mean that they see it," he continued. "Few of those who are born again in these times are opening their new eyes, their spiritual eyes. Few who are coming here now have seen the kingdom. It is a marvel that any get this far with so little vision. This is why so few are making it through even part of the wilderness.

"The Lord gave the warning, '*Woe to those who nurse babes in these times*', or 'Woe to those who keep their people in immaturity'. His warning was true—this is the great tragedy of your time."

"I know this is true. I have been preaching it for years," I agreed.

"Yes. You have, but what have you done about it?" he asked.

"I guess not much. Not as much as I should have," I confessed.

"It is the tragedy of your generation to have brought in the greatest harvest of the age, but then lost most of it. There is an even greater ingathering coming, and this must not happen again.

"There is great rejoicing at a single sinner that repents, and there is great lamentation when a single one falls away. There are not many true disciples because there are not many true shepherds. You have excelled at making converts, but you are not making them into His disciples. The Great Commission is to make disciples. The Lord gave a definition of what a disciple is, and we have few who make it even this far because you are not making disciples. This is the bane of your age."

"I am guilty," I confessed. "I knew better, and even grieved over this, but did not do much about it."

"This is why the judgment of teachers is even more severe," said the Voice. "Your shepherds have been feeding themselves and have not taken care of the people. Now the final battle is near. We have an army where even its leaders do not know how to fight. Right now few could even survive the first attack. There are already many needless casualties because of this."

"How will we win?" I asked. "We do win. It is written."

"We will win because of our Captain, but this battle is for His people. He has already won. Now you must win. I came at the beginning of the age to help prepare the way for Him then, and I have come again at the end of the age to prepare the way for Him again. I do this by helping to prepare His people. Now the first thing that must be done to prepare for Him and the times is to make the leaders into disciples. They will not know how to make disciples if they have not been disciples.

"No one can make it on this path who is not a disciple, and they certainly won't last long in the battle without being one. There should be multitudes that are on this path now, but there are few.

"You are the generation that was given the greatest resources, the most knowledge, the most freedom, but so few have come to the knowledge of the truth. Where are the shepherds?" the Voice lamented.

"I am guilty of everything you're saying," I confessed. "I have been a poor teacher, and an even worse shepherd."

"You have judged yourself rightly. Because you have judged yourself, you will not have to be judged, but you must repent. True repentance brings change.

"'*The last shall be first,*' the Voice continued. "The generation emerging is called to be the greatest of all. Right now, it is in the worst shape of all. This happened on your watch. Even so, '*where sin abounds grace does that much more abound.*' There is still grace available to change this if you repent."

"You are the one who prepares the way for the Lord. You are here to prepare us for Him. How can we make this great change? The fabric of Christianity in our time is very thin. We are as weak and unprepared as you say. What do we need to do?" I begged.

"As I said, the next step is the next step on this path. This path will prepare you, and I will help you. I was with John the Baptist to do this in his time. It begins with repentance. You cannot stay long on this path without a strong foundation of repentance. You must be quick to see your sin—quick to see your mistakes and to correct them. You are quick to see your sin and mistakes. This is helpful, but you have not been quick to correct them, and that can be your doom. Repentance is more than feeling sorry for your sin, it is turning from the sin.

"Only a foundation of repentance will keep you humble enough to walk in the grace of God. Humility is to be teachable and dependent on the Holy Spirit. This has not been a foundation that many have built upon in your time. You must start with preaching and teaching repentance. You must start praying for the Spirit to come to convict of sin. Your generation hardly even knows what sin is.

"I prayed for the judgment of God to come upon my own nation. Then I had to challenge the false teachers and prophets of my time. This is a basic duty of the prophets. Where are your prophets? Where are your apostles? Where are the shepherds who will protect God's people from the great deception of your time? Why are the wolves allowed to devour God's people right in front of them and they do nothing?

"I was taken up so that I would not see death so that I could return to prepare the way for the Lord. The Baptist loved the people enough to warn them. He loved them enough to risk his life to tell them the truth and to stand for the truth that could set them free. Where are those that can be used to prepare the way for the Lord in your time? Where are those who will even risk being rejected for the sake of the truth?"

"There are some," I replied, "but not many. They are not well known because not many will listen to them, but there are some."

"We do not need many. If they have courage and a resolute heart, it will be enough. If they have courage and a resolute heart, they will find this path," the Voice continued.

"Many think they are on the path of life, but have long ago departed from it. Only with the foundation of repentance can one find and stay on this path. Where the foundation of repentance is strong, there will be a victory over sin, not just remorse about it. The deadly trap for your generation is that they hardly know what sin is, much less how to turn from it."

"Everything you say is true," I admitted. "I may be the chief of sinners in this time. I have taken comfort that I have not committed the major sins since I have believed, but I have committed one that is worse. I have seen the Lord. I have seen His glory and His throne, and I have still become lukewarm. I have become frivolous and wasteful of my time. I should be walking in much more than I am, but as you witnessed, I did not even have enough spiritual sense to seek the living water in the wilderness.

"I know I have fallen far short of the devotion that the Lord deserves from me. This is the most difficult part of all—I am the most zealous for the Lord that I know of, and I am lukewarm. The King deserves better.

"You are right to be disappointed that I was not stronger when I got here, but it may not get much better with others who come. They may all arrive here in bad shape, but they will listen to you. They will repent, and they will walk this path with great courage."

"You are right in your judgment of yourself and your generation. The flock of the Lord is in very bad shape. As Jeremiah lamented, the sheep have become lost sheep because their shepherds have led them astray by making them turn aside to the mountains and hills, to things that will keep them excited and keep them moving. They are being led to the things of the Lord, but not to the Lord Himself. Many are now lukewarm because they have so much, so many distractions. Others are lukewarm because they are worn out from all the hype and continuous running to and fro.

"You are right about your generation. Even so, the biggest victories can only come with the biggest battles. Your generation has failed, but it does not have to end in failure. Those who repent will be given the grace to change. Then they will be given one of the greatest honors of the ages— they will be allowed to fight in the last battle. All of the prophets and righteous ones have been waiting to see these days. You are living them.

"I was surprised by the condition that you, and the few who have made it this far, have come in. But now I see strength. If the others who come have this and can keep it, then you will prevail."

"What is that strength?" I asked.

"You are quick to repent. You are not afraid of an accurate evaluation of yourself. You do not try to hide your faults or make excuses for them. That is a foundation that victory can be built upon. Only with this accurate evaluation will you fully embrace the cross as your hope. The power of God is the cross, and those who live the life of the cross will live in power.

"To be changed into the image of the Lord, you must see His glory with an unveiled face. Excuses are the biggest veil that keep people from seeing Him as He is, and from seeing themselves as they are. Those with this veil do not change. Even if they see His glory it is distorted through the veil they wear, so they are not changed by it. If you keep this humility it will not take long to get you ready for your purpose."

"What is my purpose?" I inquired.

"You are a forerunner of the forerunners. You are to help prepare those who will prepare the way for the King. They are the mighty ones that have been prophesied since Enoch spoke of them. They are alive now. This is their time, and you are called to help prepare them."

"Since Enoch did not see death, does he also have a part in preparing the way for the Lord?" I asked.

"After the Fall, Enoch was the first to recover the most basic purpose of man—to walk with God. The message of

Enoch has been for every generation. He too was taken up as a testimony that this is the victory over death—to walk with God. To walk with God is to eat of the Tree of Life. The mighty ones he was shown that come at the end of the age were given their authority because they will walk with God as Enoch did.

"Enoch has a special part in these times. Those who stay on this path and make it to the city of God do so because they learn what Enoch learned. After you have learned from me you must learn from him. Those who do not learn repentance first almost all fall to pride. The worst pride can be thinking you are closer to the Lord than others. Repentance has to come to prepare the way for the Lord so that you can walk with Him and not stray."

The Voice then motioned for me to follow him on the path. I followed. The living water and the thrill of the journey made me feel young again. I was thankful to have been able to talk to someone about the poor leader, teacher, and shepherd I had been. I knew it was true, and this gave me hope. I had the exuberance of starting over again, knowing I was being given another chance. I had found grace. I wondered if there could be any gift more wonderful than being given another chance.

As if listening to my thoughts, the Voice turned and said, "The gift of being born again is the great gift. It is the gift of starting over."

"Very true," I acknowledged. "I feel that I'm being given a whole new beginning again, almost like I'm being born again, again. Even if I failed again it would be better to die trying, to die in this wilderness, than to not try at all."

"The Lord gave us day and night so that we could wake up each day to a new day. Every day is a new beginning.

Repentance is waking up again to a new day," the Voice explained.

I was awake like I had not felt for years, and maybe ever. I was on the path again to the greatest adventure one can have in this life, seeking the city that God is building.

## CHAPTER TWO

# THE CALL

I walked in silence behind the Voice for a good distance. Gradually the path got broader so I pulled up beside him. I had many more questions and did not want to waste whatever time I had with him.

"I would like to ask you about the 'mighty ones' Enoch prophesied of," I began.

"You may ask anything," the Voice responded.

"Will these 'mighty ones' be like Enoch and walk so closely with the Lord that they will be taken up?"

"The questions you have about them would be better asked of Enoch, but I will tell you what I do know," he responded. "These 'messengers of power' will walk with the Lord like Enoch, and they will reveal His power like I did.

"Enoch was a sign. He was kept so that he would not see death for the same reason that I was—to prepare the way for the Lord by preparing His people. That Enoch walked with God and 'was not' was more than him just being caught up to heaven. He loved God so much that God became his life. He lived to know and serve the Lord. So it will be with these 'mighty ones' that he prophesied would come at the end of this age.

"I had the power, but Enoch had the greatest love for God. Enoch loved God so much that he wanted God more than he wanted food, water, or even air to breathe. Loving God is the highest purpose of man, and those who love are transformed and translated into the heavenly realms of God. At the end of this age, His messengers will have both the love for God that Enoch had and the power that I had. Their power will be the power of the love of God."

"Will I see Enoch too?" I asked.

"Those who walk this path will see me and Enoch. You must see us to stay on the path."

"So I will literally see Enoch?"

"Why do you care about what you call 'literal'? What you see in the natural is not as important or as 'literal' as what you see with the eyes of your heart, your spirit. Only love can enable you to handle the power that is to be given to God's messengers in these times without it causing you to stumble or drift from the path of life."

The Voice stopped, turned, and took hold of both of my shoulders while looking me straight in the eyes, and said,

"Love combined with power results in courage. Courage is the result of loving others more than yourself. The greatest courage comes from loving God even more than we love ourselves. If we love Him we will also love His people. You must know your message and your purpose, but those alone will not keep you. All will eventually quit if they do not have love.

"Those who have love without power will fail because true love is not just a feeling, but an action. Those who have the truth will quit if they do not love the truth. It is not just love or power, but it is the power of love you must have. Love is the greatest, but true love is expressed in power. When both are present they produce courage, because love will face trials or any danger for those they love. Where you are going you will face the greatest trials and the greatest dangers. To walk this path will take the greatest courage, so you must seek the greatest love and the power of that love."

"No one can see God and not love Him," I said.

"How do you know that?" the Voice retorted.

"I've seen Him," I answered.

"You have been given grace," the Voice responded. "No man can see Him and not be drawn to Him, except for the sons of perdition. They too are maturing in these times, and their power comes from the evil one. They will be as consumed with evil as the 'messengers of power' will be consumed with God. This is the time when good and evil will both be fully revealed on the earth."

"I have seen this too," I responded. "The Scriptures are clear that this must come, but I have not been sure of the time. It is close then?"

"It is close," the Voice acknowledged with a tremble that told me I had touched a nerve.

"There is much to do to prepare," I offered.

"'Prepare' is the crucial word for this hour," the Voice responded. "The children of light have never been further from being ready for what is coming upon them. Never have we had more to do and less time to do it in. It is good that we serve a God that does His greatest works when it becomes impossible for us. We are, therefore, about to see His greatest works."

"Those who can see are all saying this. Our hope is that when Israel fell into its darkest times then the Lord raised up His greatest prophets," I responded, pondering how the one I now walked beside had been one of these.

"Man was created to have a special relationship with God. Therefore, nothing can satisfy the heart of man like God Himself. Of the great works we are about to witness, none will be more wonderful than His presence among His people. He is going to come to His people. God's glory will be seen by His people, and His glory will appear upon them. This is what is going to draw the nations to His light," the Voice declared as if he was not only speaking to me.

"You have seen Him, and that is what has kept you. That is what has brought you to this path. Others have not seen Him with their physical eyes as you have, but they have seen Him with their hearts. They too will walk this path with courage and resolute hearts. The glory that will soon be manifested will cause everyone on earth to enter the Valley of Decision where they must choose.

"No man can see Him and not be drawn to Him, unless they are the sons of perdition that the enemy has completely taken over. There are many like this who will also be revealed. Those will only hate Him more the more they see Him. Is that not how they reacted to Jesus when He walked the earth?

"The immature believe that if those who oppose could just see a miracle they would come to the Lord. The greater the works that Jesus did the more those who served evil hated Him," the Voice stated. "Before the nations come to the light they must see the conflict between the light and the darkness once again.

"I had to stand against great evil in my time. The great evil in my time was built on religious zeal. The false prophets and teachers would cut themselves, beat themselves, and even sacrifice their own children out of zeal for the gods they served. These are the ones who think that God will only answer them when they have sacrificed enough. You are just beginning to face the same perverted religious zeal in your times. You must face it with the truth that God's own sacrifice was enough, and He will answer us because of His sacrifice, not ours.

"The harvest that is the end of this age is the time when all the seeds that have been sown come to full maturity. All that has been sown in man will now mature. The ultimate conflict of man is the one that began with the first two brothers, and this began with the sacrifice. Cain brought the fruit of his own works, and Abel brought the blood from the sacrifice of the lamb. This remains the point of all the conflict that has unfolded, and that will soon culminate in the last battle.

"You must do the same in your time that I did in my time—you must confront the false religions, the false worship, and all that is based on the works, sacrifices, and self-righteousness of men. You must confront it by standing on the works of God. The cross is your message. It is the banner that those who serve the Lord, and not just themselves, will gather under."

"I have seen how self-sacrifice can lead to self-righteousness. I have watched it turn devoted followers of the

Lord into those who cause divisions and oppose the Holy Spirit," I commented.

"There are religious conservatives who love the truth. Nicodemus and Joseph of Arimathea are examples. Such as these can be some of the pillars of the faith and will be a great strength in these times. Even so, it was the conservative religious leaders that were the resolute enemies of the Truth Himself when He walked the earth. So it will be in these times.

"Those who use religion for personal gain or position will be of special use to the enemy. There are those in high positions in religious institutions who love God, but it is a rare soul that can keep from being corrupted by religious systems. There is no greater transgression or corruption of heart than to use the things of God to draw worship or devotion to yourself. This was how Satan's fall began, and it continues to be what causes the most destructive falls of all—the fall from a high position. The higher you are when you fall the more people that will be hurt by it. When you think that this cannot happen to you, then you are in the most danger.

"To guard your heart against this you must understand the message of Enoch. Those who are walking with God, who are seeing His glory, cannot bear the thought of doing something so profane as using the things of God to draw attention to themselves. Self-promotion is not possible for those who 'are not,' because they have lost themselves in Him. Self-promotion reveals a basic delusion. It would be like the donkey Jesus rode into Jerusalem thinking all of the adulation was for it," the Voice continued.

"The same is true of churches, ministries, or any religious institution that builds on self promotion for advancement. Those that have been built on self-promotion rather than by the Holy Spirit will be some of the most deadly enemies of the truth in these times. Such advancement is the opposite of the way of true discipleship, the way of the cross, and this path that you are on now.

"It is my purpose," the Voice continued, "to challenge all who are hesitating between opinions. It is my purpose to make the opposing positions clear. That is one way that you, and all who come here, will prepare the way for the Lord in this time. The world is entering the Valley of Decision, and all must choose between the light and the darkness. It has been a basic purpose of the evil one to blur all distinctions that God has made. However, those distinctions are about to be made clear by the messengers of power, and all will be forced to choose."

"For you to be here now, the Lord's return is obviously near," I said.

"His coming is near," the Voice replied while picking up the pace, "and there is much to be done."

"You said that my destination is my home. How will going to my home help to prepare the way for the Lord?" I asked.

"Your home is His home. Your destination is the mountain. The mountain of the Lord is your home. Your home is where He is."

"You also said we were going to the city of the Lord."

"We are. His city is a city set on a hill. We are going to the mountain of the house of the Lord. That is the true home of all who love Him and do His will."

"I've been to the mountain. I had some of the greatest experiences of my life there. It has now been almost twenty years since I was there. Has anything changed since I was there?" I inquired.

"Everything changes with time except for the King," the Voice answered. "I know you have fought on the mountain. You climbed it and beheld the glory of the Lord. You have even seen what is in the heart of it, the heart of His kingdom, which is His sacrifice. Even so, there is much more to the mountain than you have seen."

"Please, tell me how has it changed?" I asked.

"Throughout this age, the mountain has been in continuous battle. It is always under assault from the enemy because it is the greatest threat to his domain. The mountain is also growing just as Daniel foresaw, but you will recognize it. Through these years since you were there you have been helping to build it."

"How is that?" I inquired.

"You helped some of the builders on their way to the mountain. You have helped more than you know to find the mountain, and they have been busy with the work of the Lord. You have more friends there than you realize," the Voice said.

"That is encouraging. In recent years I have had many failures with the ones I had such hope for. It's been hard not to wonder…."

"If anything you've done has made a difference" the Voice finished my sentence.

Again, the Voice stopped, turned, and looked me straight in the eyes, which I had learned he would do before he was to say something of great importance.

"Some who you think of as great failures you will find on the mountain. Some have been diverted from the path, but they will find their way back. All that you taught them they will remember, and it will help them. When I began to feel the same way—that I was the only one left—I became useless to the Lord, and He had to remove me and give the rest of my assignment to another. Your labor has not been in vain, and you must not trust in appearances for judging success or failure. You will have to wait for the Judgment Day to know either of these."

"Thank you. I know this is true. I know this is just self-centeredness and maybe even self-pity for me to think like that," I replied.

"It is worse! To think like that will lead you into a delusion that is as deadly as any other deception. Remember that we are all total failures and, in ourselves that is all that we will be. We must seek and build on His victory and what He is building. If we look at what He is doing we will always be encouraged, and always rejoicing. If we look at ourselves, we will always be depressed. Don't go there again. It is a departure from this path. It is what cut me off from my own purpose, and it will cut anyone off who falls to it," the Voice continued emphatically.

"I see this, but what about self-evaluation? Didn't Paul write that we should test ourselves to be sure that we are in the faith? Aren't we told to judge ourselves lest we be judged?" I asked.

"There is a place for guarding your own heart and for being watchful over your own soul, but would you want your evaluation of yourself or the Holy Spirit's evaluation?"

"The Holy Spirit's, of course," I answered.

"There are many things that are obvious that we should be able to judge easily about ourselves. What we can do we are expected to do. The deep things we must leave to the Holy Spirit. What the mature learn is to seek the conviction of the Holy Spirit, to want His correction, and to become ever more sensitive to Him. As Solomon wrote, the wise love correction. The mature take correction as evidence of God's love for them, not rejection.

"The self-pity that you have slipped into at times, and that I stumbled over, is rooted in rejection. Rejection is a deadly enemy because it is a basic deception. Your God will never reject you. He will never leave or forsake you. That is the truth you must never let go of."

We walked on for a while in silence. I felt like I had gone through deliverance. I knew everything he said, and I had taught most of it. However, I knew I had come very close to falling because I had drifted from some of the truths I had been so adamant about in my own teachings. I thought about how the Apostle Paul had told Timothy to pay attention to his own teachings, and how I needed to do the same. If I had not gotten back on this path when I did, I would very likely have stumbled just like Elijah had. I would have ended up useless for the purposes of God, and maybe even opposing them. I was overwhelmed by God's grace.

After a time, the Voice continued his instructions.

"The mountain will soon be the focus of the whole earth," he began. "Soon, all who are not building it will be seeking to destroy it. The mountain of the house of the Lord will soon challenge everyone on earth. The ultimate battle is close at hand, and the mountain will be the battlefield. You must lead all who come to this path to the mountain. They must find their place on it. That is how you will help prepare the way for the Lord."

"I have been fighting battles my whole life," I offered. "Most of them have been with myself, as you have again helped me to see. I would much rather be fighting for the mountain. Fighting on the mountain was hard. Climbing it was hard. Seeing what was in the heart of it was hard, but it was also the best time of my life. I am so glad to be going back!"

"The battles you fought with yourself were also important. If you had not fought those, you would not be here now," the Voice explained.

The path continued to get wider as we walked. I was about to ask about this when we broke out of the forest into the open. There was a beach in front of us, and a large luxury cruise ship was offloading passengers nearby. The place felt familiar, and then I recognized it as the same place from which I had entered the wilderness before.

"What are we doing back here?" I asked. "I thought we were on the path to the mountain?"

"This is the path to the mountain," the Voice said, pointing to the place where I had entered before.

"I know, but I have already been through that part of the wilderness, and I sure do not want to go through it again. Did we just walk in a big circle? Did I fail the test of this wilderness so that I must go through it again?"

"You did not fail. This is the next test, and it is a bigger one. You cannot go further until you have brought others as far as you have gone."

"So I must go through the same trials again?"

"Yes, but they should be much easier for you this time, though the journey will likely be more difficult."

"How will the trials be easier, but the journey more difficult?" I asked.

"It will be easier because you will not forget to drink the living water. It will be harder because you will have these with you," the Voice said, pointing to those getting off of the ship.

I turned to ask the Voice another question, but he was gone. As I stood there looking at the people getting off, an officer of the ship began to walk toward me, followed by a few dozen people.

"We are ready to go," the young officer said.

CHAPTER THREE

# THE CHOICE

I looked at the young officer and then at all the other passengers. Hundreds were on the beach, and I assumed that several thousand more were on the ship.

"You said you were ready to go. Where are you ready to go to?" I asked the young officer who seemed to be representing the group.

"We're going to the same place every sojourner has sought—the city that God is building."

"How do you know me, and why do you think I can take you there?" I inquired.

"We know who you are, and we were told that you know the path that will take us there," one of the passengers said.

"Are these the only ones coming?" I asked.

"The rest said they would come later," another replied.

"There may not be a later," I said. "The time is getting short."

"I've been telling them that, but they don't believe me," stated the young officer.

"What about the captain of the ship? Has he not been telling them?"

"Sir, I don't think he believes the time is short," the young officer said with the obvious agreement of those who had followed him.

"What are they going to do?" I asked. "Where are they going now?"

"They said they have everything they need. If they do not stay here, they may just cruise up and down the coast, which is what we've been doing for a long time," another one of the passengers added.

I told the group to enter the forest by the path nearby, and I would join them shortly. I knew that it was important for them to get started right away, and that if they stayed in that place long, many would be tempted to go back to the ship. I then asked the young officer to take me to the captain so I could speak to him, which he agreed to do.

As we boarded the ship, I was in awe of how beautiful it was. Everything was designed for comfort and luxury. There was a large gathering going on in the center of the ship that I could hear echoing throughout. The music was beautiful.

"You must have a great sound system on this ship," I commented to the young officer.

"Only the best. Everything is state of the art," he replied.

"Are the cabins as nice as the common areas?" I asked.

"Some are even nicer. You should see where the leaders live. They say that they must have such places to impress and entertain all of the dignitaries who visit us. We do have many famous people coming and going," the young officer added. "I was offered a magnificent place myself if I stayed."

"Were you not tempted to take it?" I asked.

"I was very tempted. Even coming back here is not easy," he answered.

"Remember that God does not tempt us. If it is temptation, we must resist it," I said, concerned that I should not have put him back in that situation, but knowing I had to speak to the captain.

"Don't worry about me," the young officer replied. "I could not abandon those who are going to the mountain. I love them more than I love this ship."

As we came to the captain's quarters, I could not help but marvel at its opulence. He was waiting to usher us in and had refreshments ready. I assumed he had been notified that I was coming when I passed the officer of the deck. He seemed genuinely glad to see me. After exchanging greetings, and some news about a few common people we knew, I got right to the point.

"Captain. I am honored that you have trusted me with some of your people to carry on this mission," I began.

"I am so happy for you to take them. They are all great people, and I think they will do very well with you," the captain replied.

"The few minutes that I was with them they seemed well prepared. My concern is for the others here. The time is short. Those who do not make this journey soon may never have the chance. This could be the last call," I stated.

"I appreciate your zeal," the captain replied, "but people have been saying that for generations. In fact, I think every generation has felt the same way, and yet time goes on."

"Even if we have a lot of time left, we do not have any time to waste. The battles between light and darkness are increasing, and the last battle is obviously near. We must make it to the mountain of the Lord with as many as we can," I urged.

"There are certainly great battles being fought," the captain replied. "We appreciate all who are fighting them and do as much as we can to support them. I have fought in quite a few myself, but right now we are being taught how to prosper. We must be obedient to our calling. This is our part now, and with our prosperity, we can help support those who are going on these missions."

The opulence and luxury were mind-numbing. Everything the captain said seemed so reasonable. My own words seemed empty and unreal on such a great ship. After the hardship I had just endured the temptation to just stop and relax on that ship for a while was very strong. The captain seemed to sense my growing weakness, and continued:

"I learned a long time ago that you have to release those who are determined to make the journey you are taking them on. If they do not go they will end up sowing discord here. They're all good people though, and I thank you for taking them.

"Before you go," the captain said, taking my forearm in a friendly gesture, "are you sure that you should not stay here for awhile? I have a perfect position for you. There is not a better place to get healed of your wounds and the hardship you have been through than right here."

I don't remember ever being so tempted in my life. I knew that if I even opened my mouth to debate with the captain, I could end up staying. I just shook my head and left as quickly as I could.

The young officer was right behind me. I felt defeated. Not only had I not been able to penetrate the atmosphere on that ship and warn those on it, it had almost taken me over. I was running for my life like a puppy with its tail between its legs.

As we crossed the beach, I turned to the young officer, "What caused you to be willing to leave such a comfortable position to strike out into a wilderness like this?"

"I don't want to be negative or disrespectful of my captain," the young officer replied. "He taught me so much and has given me so much, but all we talk about anymore is money and stuff. I signed up to serve the Lord, not to get rich. This may be what they are called to, but it is not what I am called to."

I marveled at the young man for being so resolute about something that I was so weak in. As we walked he continued:

"As great as it was to be on that ship, my heart was empty, and I was getting emptier. I saw good people drifting, beginning to do things that should not be done. I knew that if I did not leave that ship very soon I never would. Then I would live a life of compromise and defeat. I think this was my last call regardless of how much time the world has."

"You do know that you are leaving this luxury and comfort for great hardship, don't you?" I asked.

"Yes, I do know that. It may be more difficult than I think, but I have been reading the classics, the great messengers of the Lord in history. They all lived a very different life than we were living on that ship. The more I read about the lives of the great saints the more I questioned everything we were doing and teaching. I could not bear it any longer. The captain was right. I would have caused discord if I had stayed. I have to make this journey or I will never be at peace," the young officer confided.

"You have done the right thing," I said, "but it will be hard. How about the people who followed you, do they know what they are getting themselves into?"

"They were all part of a group we started called 'The Society of Bonhoeffer,'" the young officer said.

"I guess that says enough," I replied as we entered the wilderness. I noticed that he did not even look back at the ship.

The young officer and I had not gone very far before it became too dark to proceed. We found a stream of the living water nearby, refreshed ourselves, and went to sleep. When we woke we drank from the stream, prayed, and then started down the path at a quick pace. It took us much longer than I expected to catch up to the group from the cruise ship that had gone before us.

The group had not only pressed ahead with resolve, but they had not drifted from the path. None had wandered off alone and gotten lost. I had not done that well when I was alone and was impressed with them. I was relieved that this seemed to be a group that would not need micromanaging.

When we got to the group, they were exhausted but cheerful. I asked if they had found water or food. A smart looking middle-aged man with a designer haircut said they had not. They were thirsty, maybe more thirsty than they had ever been. I knew this would be good for them. Now they would really appreciate the living water.

I asked the man who had answered me for his name. He only gave his first name, William. I then asked if he had a wife. He said that he was no longer married, and volunteered that his wife had left him. I expressed my condolences, and then asked if that was why he came on this journey. His reply was illuminating.

"I would not say that her leaving me had nothing to do with it," he answered, "but I think she left me more because I had lost my vision, my purpose, more than just for another man. My life had become empty, and I was becoming bitter. I don't blame her for leaving me. I did not even like myself until I found this group."

"So how did you learn about this path?" I inquired.

"Some of these here saw how empty and alone I was and asked me to come to their little fellowship. I was so desperate at the time that I would have tried anything, so I went. They talked about the dreams some had of a mountain that was like the mountain of the Lord. They believed we were called to that mountain. I thought it was all foolishness at first, but there was more life in their foolishness than I had experienced in a long time, so I kept coming to the meetings. Finally, I decided that it would be better to die seeking that mountain than to live the way that I had been living. I got caught up in their vision. It may be foolishness, but I have hope again like I have not had for many years. I know now that the greatest treasure I could ever find is purpose, and now that I have it again I would rather die than lose it."

I surveyed the group and could tell that William was very different from the rest. He was obviously not just a professional, but likely a high achiever. Feeling that he had more to say I asked him to continue, so he did:

"I have also come to love these people like my own family. I have had presidents and other great and powerful people seek my counsel, but I have sought the counsel of these here. I have never found the kind of heart, the greatness of spirit, or wisdom like I have found with these people. I would rather be in their fellowship than with any of the great ones in this world. I would rather be in this wilderness with them, seeking this mountain they speak of, than live in any palace."

The others were looking at William as if they had never heard this from him before, so I asked how well they knew William. Some said that they knew that his wife had left him, but that was all. He had obviously been very quiet in their fellowship, but was now opening up. This was a positive sign. They were already bonding on a new level.

I asked William to choose several scouts to send out in pairs in different directions to look for water. I instructed them not to go beyond shouting distance from where we were. They found water quickly. It was close by, just as the Voice had said it would always be.

After everyone had quenched their thirst, I gathered the group together to give them a briefing on our journey. They were intent, focused, and almost bursting with energy. The effect of the water was obvious.

"I went back to see your captain and the ship," I began. "I am impressed that you could leave all of that to strike out into this wilderness. We have heard William's reasons for doing this, but I would like to hear from some of the rest of you why you would do this."

One of the older women spoke up, "We have not had this water for a long time. Just one drink is worth leaving all of that."

The others agreed.

"This is the living water," I said. "You are right. There is no treasure on earth that can compare to it. Even so, I'm still impressed that you would leave all that you had not really knowing what you would find. You are already great saints in my book."

"To leave anything we know, to strike out into the unknown, takes great faith, but it takes an uncommon faith to leave all that you did to make such a journey," someone said from behind me. I turned to see the Voice.

Who are you?" one of the group asked him.

He did not answer, but rather nodded for me to continue. He was of such an unimpressive, unobtrusive demeanor that I quickly had their attention again.

"I don't think I have ever seen such luxury and comfort as on the ship you left. That you left so much was a great sacrifice, and sacrifice is what will get you through this wilderness to your destination. The mountain is real. I have been there. You have never seen glory like you will see on that mountain, but neither have you seen battle and conflict like you will experience there.

"It will not be an easy journey, but it will be worth it. That you had what it takes to begin means you also have what it takes to finish, if you do not get distracted from the path. There are many traps intended to get us off the path. Some are deceptive, and all are enticing, but they will all result in getting you so lost that it will be difficult for you to find the path again.

"This wilderness is hostile to us in every way. It is dangerous, and many do not make it through. It is probable that you will now face the greatest trials you have ever faced in an environment that is trying every way it can to stop you. I know you called yourselves 'The Society of Bonhoeffer.' That is fitting, because you will need to draw on the kind of courage and focus that he had for this journey."

A young lady spoke up, "We will not be easily turned back. We have all experienced what it is like to live without a great purpose. It is better to die as Bonhoeffer did than to not walk the path we have been called to. Death is not the worst thing that can happen to us."

"What is your name?" I inquired.

"Mary."

When she spoke I could tell that many looked at Mary with affection and respect, even though she was young, maybe in her early twenties. Then another one in the group said,

"Mary has a double portion of curiosity," which the others quickly affirmed with their laughs. Mary seemed not to notice.

"So Mary has a lot of questions, which keeps everyone else seeking answers. Good, we need that," I said.

"That you are here means you have heard the call, and you made the choice to obey it. It is one of the most important choices you have ever made. As Bonhoeffer once wrote, 'When the Lord calls a man, He bids him to come and die.' You are about to experience the truth of that, but you will also know the truth of what the Lord said, that if we lose our life for His sake we will find it. You will die some every day, but you are now on the greatest adventure that one can have in this life."

And so the journey began.

## CHAPTER FOUR

# THE PATH

Mary had questions because she wanted answers. She was not just seeking attention. In fact, she was so confident that I could tell that she did not need or want the attention or deference the others gave her. She wanted the truth. I could also sense that I was about to be subjected to her tests to see if I was qualified to be their leader. This was interesting to me because when I had met them on the beach they had somehow known that I was to be their leader.

"It seems that you are well prepared for this journey," I said to the group. "I have made it through this part of the wilderness, and I want to share with you how I did it. I did not do everything right, and some of the things I did we don't want to repeat, but I think we can learn from them so as not to make those mistakes again. My goal is to get you through this part as fast and as safely as possible, while learning everything we're here to learn.

"I think one of the things that helped me most was to reckon myself as dead. I not only resolved to take up the cross and die to my own wants and even my needs, I considered that every day would be my last, and I would very likely die that day. The last few days I did not have to imagine this, I really thought that death was likely, the journey had become so difficult."

"That's a bit melodramatic, isn't it?" someone in the back remarked.

"I think it would be if it were not true." I answered. "There is an advantage to this. As I was saying, we are likely to experience things ahead that make us think it really will be our last day in this life. Considering yourself as already dead to this world makes it much easier to face this. If we live or die, we are the Lord's. If the fear of death starts to control us we will not make it through.

"There is another way this can help us. When you consider that every day might be your last it brings a focus to your life so that you live more every day than you may ever have before. That enables us to get the most out of every day, which is one of the purposes of the wilderness. When we are threatened with death we begin to live like never before."

As I surveyed the group, I was encouraged by how they listened so intently. The art of listening had become rare in our times, but this group was different. I knew the living water had a lot to do with their present mental sharpness, but they seemed exceptionally clear and resolute for this journey. The Voice leaned over and whispered to me:

"Vision is what you are seeing. They would not be sojourners if they were not people of exceptional vision. This helps to give them their focus. You must have uncommon vision to even hear the call to come here."

As Elijah motioned for me to continue, I did:

"If we walk in fear, we are almost certain to fall. We are going to need more faith and more of the peace of God in our hearts for the battles ahead of us. Fear will cause us to make the wrong choices. If we are already dead to this world what can the world do to us? A dead man has nothing to fear. If we have truly died with Christ, we will be raised with Him, so we should have no fear, even of death. We must live by faith and be guided by faith, not fear, to stay on the right path.

"I did not want to die, but when I died to my own life I began to really live. When I got my focus off myself, off my needs, and on to what I was supposed to be learning, I began to cherish every day as the gift that it is. Render yourself dead now and it will be much easier for you. Those who live this way are the freest of all people. He who is dead needs nothing. As a great saint once said, 'He who stands in need of nothing cannot be bound by anything.'

"It is those who are dying daily that are the most alive. This living water is the sweetest to them and the most powerful. Death is the path to true life, and dying to self is how we stay on the path of life.

"There is another more important reason why we must reckon ourselves as dead. This is the commandment of the Lord for His disciples. When He said that if we seek to save our lives, we will lose them, but if we will lose them for His sake, we will find them, He was giving us one of the great keys to true life. We lay down our lives for Him because He deserves this devotion. He deserves a people who will be obedient in all things, and this is basic to being His disciple."

After a moment someone in the group asked, "Who is your friend?"

I turned and looked at the Voice. I saw him shake his head so slightly that I was probably the only one who could see it, but I knew I could not tell them yet.

"He is a friend of yours, too," I responded. "We will be seeing a lot of him, and you will get to know him well in due time. I need to speak to him alone for a few minutes, and it is time for you to get going. I'll catch up with you shortly."

With that, the group started out. After they had passed out of hearing, the Voice began:

"I've come to talk to you about William and Mary. Anyone who has made it this far on the path is a person of exceptional faith and vision, but these two are among the most exceptional I have seen for a very long time. I was told there are others like them in this group as well. They will also be your biggest trials. Keep in mind that they are worth it for what they can ultimately become. I was sent to warn you of a trial that will come through Mary that can also jeopardize your whole group."

"What kind of trial?" I asked.

"It's not what you think. She does know very well how to use her beauty. The world taught her that at a very young age, but that is not the main trial you will face with her. Mary has questions that you must answer. They are questions that almost all think about, but very few consider them as important as she does. They are important questions, and they need to be answered, not just for her sake, but for the sake of all who are with you."

"Will you answer them?" I asked.

"No. You will."

"Do I have the answers? I don't even know what the questions are."

"One of the reasons why you were chosen to lead this group is because you had the same questions at one time, and you kept asking them until you found the answers. It is not just giving the right answers to Mary's questions that are important, but how you answer them."

With that the Voice looked me sternly in the eyes, nodded, and then started walking away.

"Do you know the questions?" I called after him. "Tell me how I answer them if that is so important."

"With wisdom and patience," the Voice replied, just before he disappeared in the trees.

I walked fast to catch up with the group. This time they had not gone as far as I expected. It seems that William opening up about his life had caused others to do the same. Almost all were walking rather casually while sharing their stories with each other. I felt that this was healthy, so I slowed and decided to stay behind them and let this go on. It was not long before I was spotted.

"Okay. You have to tell us who your friend is," one of them demanded.

"Trust me, you will get to know him very well before we get out of here, but it's not time to talk about him yet," I said, as emphatically as I could to try to discourage more questions about him. It didn't work.

"That wasn't the Lord, was it?" one elderly lady chimed in.

"No." I assured her.

"Was it an angel?" another asked.

"I hate to disappoint you, but he is not an angel. I will tell you as much as I can at the right time, if he does not do it himself," I said as firmly as I could without being rude.

"I was listening to your conversation as I caught up with you. One of the most important purposes of this wilderness is to forge the greatest fellowship we can have on earth—*koinonia*."

"What is that?" William asked.

"It is the Greek word used in The Bible for fellowship or communion, which means common-union. However, this is much more than the kind of fellowship or friendships we have in this world. *Koinonia* is a bonding together like the members of our body into a single, greater unit that are inseparable. It implies a bonding so deep that if we were separated it would be like having a member of your body cut off. We will have to become that close for what we are entering into. We will perish in this wilderness without it.

"As vital as this is, it is not something that we can just manufacture. We can help the process by keeping in mind that we must have this, and therefore, refuse to let anything divide us. However, there are two basic things that will forge us together as we must be. The first will be the process of experiencing this wilderness together. The second, and even more important, is growing in our love for the Lord so much that we love Him more than our own life. Then, we will always treat even the least of His people as we would treat Him, knowing how important this is to Him.

"These are the things that lead to *koinonia*. As we are told in I John 1:7, '*If we abide in the light as He is in the light, we have koinonia and the blood of Jesus will cleanse*

52

*us from all sin.'* It is written that '*the life is in the blood,*' and we must have *koinonia* for the life of Christ to flow through His body, just as the members of our body must all be connected for the life-blood to flow through them.

"For you to already be as close as you are you must have begun to taste this in your small groups on the ship. There was already such a bond that all who were experiencing it on the ship came on this journey. This place will cause you to bond even deeper. Treasure these times. Never take them for granted. Such an experience is becoming rare in Christianity, but it is essential for the fullness of Christ to be revealed through His people."

"This is not such a bad place, but I don't think I would want to go anywhere like this alone. Why did you go alone?" one of them asked.

"I couldn't find anyone at the time to go with me. That is why it was so much harder for me than it needed to be, and why I didn't get very far," I confessed.

"What do you mean you did not get very far? I thought you made it through this wilderness before," Mary spoke up.

"I have been to the mountain before, but I got there a different way. I have actually been through quite a few wildernesses though, but this one is different. All of the others seem to have just been training for this one. I only made it part of the way before I was taken back to the beginning to help you."

"That must have been hard," someone said. "Having to go back and get us after already getting through part of it."

"It was discouraging at first, but I am already thankful. I may need you more than you need me. We need each other, and it will always be easier with others," I began. "The fellowship and adventure we will experience here will make even life on the luxury cruise ship seem boring and insignificant."

Then a voice I did not recognize began to speak from behind me:

"The mighty men of Israel who served King David were fashioned into the fellowship they became through the trials they went through together. You too are being fashioned into the fellowship of warriors you are called to be in this wilderness."

I turned to see who was speaking, but did not recognize him. It was a young man who seemed about sixteen years old.

"That's a good insight," I said. "And who might you be?" I asked.

"My name is Mark. I was told I would find a company of great warriors on this path and that I was to join you."

"I would not call us that yet," I replied, "but I think we are warriors in the making."

"You must be the ones I'm seeking because this is where I was told to find you. May I join you?"

It seemed everyone chimed in at once with, "Of course you can… Please do… We are happy to have you…" Then the introductions began. Mark may not have looked very exceptional, but he did have an extraordinary presence and the demeanor of a seasoned veteran even though he was so young. The welcome he received was warm, but one got the feeling that if he had met with resistance, he would have been just as comfortable.

"Have you been to the mountain?" I asked Mark.

"No, but I have fought many battles, and it is the purpose of my life to make it to the mountain," he responded. Then he looked at me and said, "Sir, I interrupted you. I'm sorry. Please continue."

"It was a welcome interruption," I answered, "and a good example of what I was talking about. I was telling them about how facing trials together will forge us into the fellowship we are called to be. Your example of King David and his mighty men was perfect. Do you have more you can tell us about this" I asked.

"Those who have never tasted of this fellowship cannot understand it, but the bond forged in battle and adversity is like no other," Mark began.

"You are quite young, but you speak as if you have already experienced this. Tell us a little about yourself," I said.

"I am young, but I have a lot of experience. I have tasted of this kind of fellowship. Three friends and I determined when we were twelve years old that we were going to be the best disciples that the Lord ever had. The resistance we received from just about everyone, including our teachers, parents, and even our pastor, surprised and deeply hurt us, but we were determined to keep our vow.

"When we started having visions and dreams, mostly about the mountain of the Lord, we foolishly tried to share them with others. They were not ready. We were separated from each other, tested by psychiatrists, and finally sent to different boarding schools for troubled youth. Even though we were separated like this we have been able to stay in touch. I expect to meet them either on this journey or on the mountain."

"How did you get out of the school?" I inquired.

"Most were in these schools for crimes, drugs, or being in gangs. They did not take to me very well, but I was still determined to keep my vow to be the best disciple of Christ I could be. I had to escape or I do not think I would have lived much longer. Then I was told that I would find you here."

"Who told you that?" someone in the group asked.

Mark looked to me as if he needed my permission to answer this question. I nodded for him to go ahead.

"An angel told me in a dream," Mark answered.

There was silence for a long moment before Mary spoke up:

"So you saw an angel? What else did he tell you?" Mary inquired.

"He told me about some of you," Mark began. "Is your name Mary? You must be. There is no one else here that fits your description."

They were all silent for a moment as they tried to remember if anyone had called her "Mary" since Mark had joined them. They were all quite sure they had not, when Mary continued:

"And what did this angel tell you about me?"

"That you have a lot of questions. Most are good, and that you will be given answers to them, but some are from a cynicism that could sidetrack you if you become impatient or arrogant," Mark said, looking Mary straight in the eyes.

Mary and everyone else knew that there was no way Mark could have known this having just met them. It was exactly what Mary needed to hear. After another long moment someone else asked:

"Did he say anything about any of the rest of us?"

"He did," Mark replied. "I wrote them down, and can share them with you. Some of these things are personal though, and I don't want to embarrass anyone. For most I would rather wait until it seems the right time. There is one person here that you should all know about, and I think it would be good to share what I was shown about him," Mark said, as he looked to me to see if he should continue.

"Please do," I said.

"There is someone here who has known many great leaders, even world leaders. He now sees himself as a failure and not a leader. He has had some failures, especially in relationships, but he is not a failure. He will be a great leader on the mountain. He will help many others become leaders and avoid the failures he has been through. In this group, he will be like a compass for us. He will be used to get us through some great difficulties in this wilderness and will help us keep going in the right direction. I was to tell him that the Lord has never been disappointed with him and that his future is bright."

Everyone looked at William, who had tears running down his face. They all knew Mark could not have known this and that it had come from above. After a few moments Mary spoke up again:

"Mark. What did the angel look like?"

Mark instinctively looked to me as to whether he should answer, which did not set well with Mary. I was pondering how important the Voice had said Mary's questions were, and that it was important how I answered them. As I paused, Mary spoke again:

"Why does he have to get your permission to answer?"

"He doesn't," I replied, "but there are some things that are sensitive and need to be shared at the right time. I appreciate Mark having the maturity to consider the counsel of others about what he is to share."

"You're right," Mary confessed. "I was out of line. I'm sorry."

"Mary, I do not want to inhibit your questions," I responded. "You have to determine if you are asking any in impatience or arrogance as Mark had the warning for you, but you need to be free to ask them.

"Nor do I want to inhibit Mark or anyone else from sharing what you think is appropriate. You all must be free to do this because you are all going to be shown things about one another that will not only be helpful, but necessary for this journey.

"As for your questions, they say the only dumb question is one that is not asked. I'm not totally convinced of that, but questions indicate caring, so I hope you and everyone else always feel free to ask them.

"I also think that Mary's question about the angel is one of the important ones that we all need to talk about. Mark, what did the angel look like?" I asked.

"He looked like a young man, maybe even my own age. I thought it was a person until he disappeared right in front of me," Mark answered, and then looked at me as if he needed some understanding of this himself.

"In Scripture we see that this is not an uncommon experience with believers, and it will be common here. We do often entertain angels and are not aware of it because most of the time they appear as just another person. I am not sure why they do this, but I suspect it is to keep from alarming us too much, which we would be if we saw them in their true form. It seems that as we mature, they do start appearing in their real form."

"Have you seen many of them?" someone asked.

"I have and you will, if you stay on this path," I continued. "They are ministering spirits who serve the heirs of salvation. Those who are on this journey will almost certainly see them, and often. In fact, you will be the exception if you don't. This is important to understand, because it is something we must get used to and not be overly infatuated with it.

"We should give honor to angels as the messengers of the Lord, but we only worship the Lord. We will have plenty of time to talk more about this, but for now I think we need to get moving again.

"Mark, we're all thankful to have you join us. Please take your liberty to share with anyone whatever you think is appropriate that you have been shown about us."

As the group started down the path, I told them I would catch up with them. I stayed behind because I had seen the Voice nearby. I knew I would not have seen him if he did not want to be seen, so I knew he had something important. I walked over to him and he began:

"I see all who take this journey, but I have never seen a group quite like this one before," the Voice said.

"I'm still wondering if that is that good or bad," I commented.

"We'll see," he responded. "One thing is for sure, it will not be boring for you! You like to say that you may die of a lot of things but boredom won't be one of them, but I think you may soon be asking for a little boredom."

"I guess we will see," I responded. "How did you know I often used that remark? I have not used it in this wilderness."

"I am but one of the 'great company of witnesses' who have been watching these times unfold and watching those of you who have been given the honor to live in them. The righteous and prophets of old desired to see these days, and they are now seeing them. You live before an audience far greater than you could imagine," the Voice replied.

"That adds even more gravity to this situation," I responded.

"If your eyes were open as they should be you would see the great host of heaven that is with you. Right now you could not bear the gravity of these times, but you will grow in stature and vision until you can," the Voice added resolutely.

"It is all I can do now to keep my attention on this group, so this is just as well I guess," I responded. "I want to get to the place where I can handle it all, but with all the years and experiences I've had, I feel almost like a new believer just starting out again. I know I have a great deal more to learn."

"This is true. You have been through much, but there is more for you to grow up into than what you have done so far. This must also be done in a much shorter period of time, so it will be intense. From now on, every day you will be stretched," the Voice said.

"I'm sure a lot of that stretching is going to come from this group," I said. "There is something very remarkable about them. I need to thank you for bringing me back for them. I did not appreciate it at the time, and I never thought I would be excited to be going through this place again, but I am very glad to be with this group. I now know that to get the full benefit of this wilderness I need to experience it with others."

"That's *koinonia*," the Voice added. "It gives us a little insight into why the Lord came to the earth for all of us. I have experienced much of heaven, but of all of God's creatures there is something remarkable and interesting about people. The Lord loves to be with us. Angels do too. One of the main attractions of man is the ability to have *koinonia*. You have a hard job ahead of you, but it can be worth it."

"I am enjoying it so far, but you don't think I'm called to be a professional wilderness guide do you?" I asked.

"No, that's my job. I'm the voice in the wilderness. Your place is on the mountain. What did you think of Mary's questions?"

"I didn't think any were out of line. I think she brings a lot of life with her questions. She is probably asking what everyone else is thinking," I answered. "Were those last ones 'the big ones' that it is so crucial that I handle rightly?"

"No, not even close, but they will be coming soon. You've only had teasers so far."

"What kind of questions could these be? Should I brush up on the free will of man versus the sovereignty of God?"

"No, they will be much more difficult than that," the Voice said, now with a distinguishable smile. "And she will not take clichés or superficial answers, and you're not to give her any. You must answer her questions. They are important to her and to others."

"And you can't tell me some of these questions so I can be prepared?" I asked.

"I don't know what they are. I just know how important they are and how important these people are. I'm curious too. This is a first for me, being sent back a second time to warn someone about the same thing," the Voice said with more gravity. "I know you have answers, but I don't think you will be able to answer them all. That's because I was told that the council is waiting to help you with them. Do not hesitate to inquire of the Lord, and He will give you wisdom."

The Voice then turned and started to walk away. I called out after him, "What else is so special about this group?"

He stopped, hesitated for a moment, and then turned and said, "I have never seen so many in one group who are called to be the mighty ones that Enoch talks about. Every one of these is called to walk in more power than I did. Obviously the time is now close."

As the Voice passed out of sight, I began walking slowly to catch up with the group. I wanted to process all that the Voice had just told me. If I had known what awaited me, I would have slowed down even more.

## CHAPTER FIVE

# THE TEST

When I caught up to the group they were sitting next to the path, obviously weary, but talking to each other. I approached slowly so as not to disturb their discussion. They were sharing their own stories. When I was spotted, they stopped and turned to me. Mary spoke up, asking what they were all wanting to know:

"Who is that man?"

"He is the Voice," I responded.

"What voice?" Mary continued.

"The Voice of the one who cries in the wilderness." I answered.

"Do you mean Elijah?" someone in the group asked.

"Yes." I answered.

There was a long silence as they pondered this. Then Mary continued her inquisition:

"You are serious?"

"I am serious."

"Will he be back?" someone else asked.

"He will never be far from us while we are in the wilderness. He is here to prepare the way for the Lord. A basic way that he does this is by working with all who travel this path," I replied, a little surprised that they all believed me so easily. I continued:

"We are on the path to another world, another realm. On this path, we begin to learn to live in two worlds—the spiritual and the natural. This can be hard at first, but these two worlds were made to be connected, to interface in many different ways. Man, who was created to fellowship with God who is Spirit, was also created to be the connector of these two worlds. To live in both worlds is, therefore, the most natural state for man. The more you can do this the more you will become who you were created to be. This is not unnatural, but the natural state of man when we are delivered from the consequences of the fall."

I looked around at their faces to try to gauge who was having trouble understanding what I was saying. To my surprise, it seemed that this was nothing new to them, so I continued:

"The Scriptures will not just come alive to us here, but we will live them. In fact, we must live them to survive. They will be our food. Man does not live by bread alone, but by every word that proceeds from the mouth of God. This is present tense, not past tense. We must receive daily bread from above, the Word of God that is living and comes from Him now, in the present.

"We can no longer merely believe that the things written in The Bible are true, but true faith in The Bible is faith to experience what is written for our present life. There is nothing written in The Bible that we cannot experience today, and we will here. Some of you will likely be used to do even greater miracles than what was done in The Bible. We are now in the times of 'the greater works' Jesus spoke of.

"Again, The Bible is not just a history book to believe, it is what we will live and the food that will sustain us every day. It is the arsenal of weapons we will use in every battle. Knowing The Bible is not just a good thing to do, but here it will mean life or death.

"This wilderness is beautiful, but deadly. It will try to kill you any way that it can, and it has a lot of ways to do it. If it does not kill you it will seek to have you turn back. As frightening as this wilderness can be fear will lead you into its traps, so fear can never become our guide. We must learn not to allow fear to control us or influence our decisions. We must use every fear that comes upon us as a chance to resist it and to grow in faith. We will have a chance to do this every day, and every day that we stay the course we will become stronger in the Lord.

"We must also use every trial of confusion to grow in wisdom. Every day it will take more faith and wisdom to stay on the right path. Wisdom comes from experience that is viewed with a teachable heart."

"How many paths are there?" someone asked.

"There are many, and they are almost all very tempting and inviting," I answered.

"How can we tell the right one?" someone else asked.

"There is no formula. There is no 'how to' that we can use. We are to follow a Person, not a formula. However, my experience has been that the right path always seems to look harder, and in fact is harder, at least for a time. It never seems to be the most inviting, which is why we must have faith to see it and follow the Lord not just our own reasoning.

"The wrong paths seem to always look easier, and will tempt us to try to escape our difficulties and trials. They may, in fact, be easier for a time, but then they will get much harder than the true path. They ultimately lead to traps and entanglements that few ever get free of, if they do not turn back quickly and get back on the right path.

"The right path may never actually get easier, but it seems to become easier as we grow stronger and wiser. The right path has one thing no other path has, and it is the greatest thing of all. When you are on the right path you will get continually closer to the Lord, and His living water will always be available. There is no greater peace and joy that we can know than being close to Him. Our closeness to Him can be so wonderful that we will begin to delight in this wilderness. With Him, the most desolate cave is better than a palace. Without Him, the greatest palace can be worse than a desolate cave.

"If you get on a wrong path, it will lead you away from Him. The joy and peace of the Lord will be replaced by confusion and darkness. '*The path of the righteous is like the light of the dawn that shines brighter and brighter until the full day.*' The path of the righteous is the right path. The right path gets brighter and brighter until we are walking in the fullness of the light. The wrong path gets darker and leads to increasing confusion. Confusion leads to depression and ultimately to despair and death.

"As your fellowship has already grown beyond what you enjoyed on the ship, it will grow much deeper here. Fighting through hardships will knit you together like few things can. There is something else that you will experience here that will create an even greater bond—you will experience the glory of the Lord together. To experience His glory and presence together is the greatest bond of all."

As I talked, I saw Elijah nearby listening to all that I was saying. This was a bit disconcerting, as well as comforting. It was disconcerting because I felt foolish talking about the wilderness with the master of the wilderness listening. It was comforting to know that he was watching over us so closely. He motioned for me to continue:

"You are all here because you were called. You were known before the world began. You have been given the opportunity to run the race for the highest prize there has ever been or ever will be. This is the path to the high calling of God that the apostles wrote about. Just by beginning, you have already joined the greatest souls to ever walk the earth. It took great faith to begin, and it will take greater faith every day to continue. It was not intended to be easy, but to be the foundry of the great ones who will reign with Christ in His kingdom."

"What about those still on the ship?" a young girl asked. "My parents are on the ship. Won't they rule with Christ also?"

"If anyone calls on the name of the Lord they will be saved, they have eternal life and a glorious eternity before them," I responded. "But this path is for those who would run the race that the Apostle Paul spoke of near the end of his life. He spoke of a better resurrection that he did not feel he had yet attained to, but that he was pressing on toward the mark of the high calling. He was not speaking there of salvation or eternal life. These he had the day he trusted the Savior for his salvation. There is a high calling that not many see and not many pursue. This is the path to '*the high calling of God in Christ Jesus.*'"

"I thought we were all going to be the same in heaven," another chimed in.

"Where did you get that from?" I asked.

"I'm not sure. I think I heard it, but I may have just assumed it. I've never before heard what you're talking about. Are you sure this is in the Scriptures?" she continued.

"Yes, this is in the Scriptures, and you are right to question this. There is much in Scripture about the high calling, and those will be illuminated and fortified in you on this journey. You need to see the high calling to walk this path, just as the Savior endured the cross for the glory that was set before Him. If He needed to see the reward how much more do we need to see it to endure the life of the cross that we have been called to?

"It is right to have this discussion here," I continued. "All of His created beings have been created for a specific purpose and place in His creation. He has given an opportunity for some from fallen mankind to become His very own family, sons and daughters of the King of kings, and to take on His divine nature. All of creation marvels at this 'new creation' that is being raised up from fallen mankind. As they witness the resolve, the sacrifice, and the character of those who walk this path and endure against such opposition and hardship all for the sake of their King, even the angels acknowledge that these are worthy to be their judges."

"But if it is all by grace, then how is it that people have different rewards, or positions, in heaven?" The young girl blurted out, obviously agitated.

"That is a good question," I tried to encourage her. "It is true that all that we are and all that we become is by the grace of God. It is by the grace of God that you were called and that you heard the call. We are also told to '*make our calling and election sure.*' This is why the Holy Spirit is called 'the Helper,' not 'the Doer.' We have a part to do also. We must accept His grace and then walk in it. '*Many are called, but few are chosen,*' or few respond to the call to make their calling and election sure.

"There is a mentality that has crept into much of the world that we are all the same, and all deserve the same, regardless of effort or accomplishments. That is not a biblical concept. In fact, it is contrary to justice, one of the two foundations of the throne of God which is the kingdom of God. The promises given to the churches in Revelation were to the 'overcomers' in those churches. Something other was promised to those who did not care enough to live what was revealed to them.

"Like it or not, understand it or not, God chooses who to give opportunities to, and then they must choose to take those opportunities. This is why it says, '*Moses chose to suffer the afflictions with the people of God esteeming the reproach of Christ as greater riches than all of the treasures of Egypt.*' You too have made a similar choice when you chose to follow this path."

I could tell that the young girl was still having trouble with this concept, but no one else seemed to. Even so, this was making her so uncomfortable that she was obviously not going to ask any more questions. I had learned that when someone has such a veil over their minds concerning a clear and basic biblical truth, no argument can remove that veil, but only the Holy Spirit. So I told them we would talk more about these things later and that we needed to get moving again.

As we began walking, the young girl pulled up beside me. "I do not mean to be impertinent," she began, "but if this is true, I want to understand it. Can I ask you more questions as we walk?"

"Of course," I replied. "You can ask me anything, if you will allow me to say 'I don't know' when I don't know the answer."

"Fair enough," she began. "I'm one of those who has always had trouble when I think about all of the people who never had a chance to even hear the gospel. So it is hard for me to hear about some who get to run the race for this glorious high calling when others don't even get salvation."

"That is a fair question," I responded, "and I think it is one that every thinking person who really cares about justice must ask. It took me many years to find an answer that satisfied me, but it is not a simple issue."

"Will you share what you learned with me?" she asked.

"I've never shared all that I learned about this with anyone because it would take so long to do it right. But I'm willing to share as much as I can with you while we are together on this journey.

"First, in anything we accept as doctrine, as a truth, it must be confirmed in the Scriptures. No opinion of man, or even angels, can carry the weight of the written Word of God. It took me years to come to my understanding of these issues and to establish them in the Scriptures. To convey in a short time is not likely, but I can help you begin down the right path to searching out the truth.

"Why don't we do this: let's take your questions one at a time, and I will share with you my conclusions and as much as I can about how I came to them. If my conclusions don't satisfy you, then ask for more, and I'll try to show you how I came to them."

"I would appreciate any help," she replied.

"What I did find through all of my searching absolutely convinced me of the righteousness and justice of the Lord, and how He even went far beyond that to add grace and mercy," I said.

"I would like to have these things settled in my heart," the young girl continued.

"Okay, but I want to tell you up front that my main purpose in sharing these things with you is to give you something that could be even better than my conclusions," I said.

"What is that?"

"The path that I took to find my answers. Sometimes it is not just the answers that are important, but how you come to the answers.

"Those that come too cheaply are not as valuable. When you work to obtain them they become treasures of wisdom and knowledge that you will value enough to take care of," I replied.

"Well, it seems that we may be together on this journey for awhile, so I'm open. What was the path that you took to find the answer to this?"

"First, what is your name?"

"I'm Mary."

"Fitting," I replied, "and that's a compliment. So we have two Mary's on this journey, and you seem very much alike. Your parents must have been prophetic. Like the Mary who was Martha's sister in the gospels, you are called to have a special relationship to Jesus."

"I hardly feel that close to the Lord. I feel that my questions may be an insult to Him. I don't mean for them to be, and I know my concern for the people I love can eclipse my devotion to the Lord at times, but I cannot shake these questions, and they are hurting my ability to trust the Lord."

The other Mary pulled closer, and spoke up, "We do share many of the same questions. I've been listening to your conversation. If that is the real Elijah, then surely he knows the answers. Can you get him to come back and talk to us?"

"Believe me, I would like to have him answer all of your questions, and I would like to hear his answers too, but I'm afraid that is not going to happen."

"Why not?" the older Mary asked.

"He told me about your questions and said that I would have to answer them. He did not know what the questions were, but he said that they were important for the entire group, and that I would have the answers," I replied.

"That's weird, that he knew about our questions, but it also sounds like God is not angry at us for having them," the younger Mary remarked.

"Of course, He's not angry. I don't think the Lord ever minds sincere questions. In fact, He has made it very clear that yours are very important," I said.

I then said to the whole group, who I could see was watching us and would like to be included in the conversation, "Let's go over to the bank by the living water and take some time to discuss some of the questions you have."

I waited for all to drink and then settle about on the rocks and ground near the stream. I then asked for volunteers to post watchmen back on the path. Then I began:

"A friend once told me that almost every heresy is the result of trying to carry to logical conclusions that which God has only revealed in part. I think this is true. At the same time, we are told that we know in part and see in part. None of us has the whole picture, or the whole understanding. So to have the whole truth we must put what we have together with what others have.

"There are some things that, if we pooled all of our knowledge together, we would still only have part of the understanding because that is all God has revealed to man at this time. That which God has only revealed in part we must not add to by trying to carry it to what we think are logical conclusions. He has His reasons for not giving us more at this time. We will have eternity to get our questions answered, so some of them need to wait. We honor Him and prove our trust for Him by accepting this. That must be acceptable to us for the walk of faith."

"Okay. I know I may not learn all there is about this matter, but some of the questions I have make it harder for me to go forward with the trust that I need," the older Mary confided while the younger Mary nodded her agreement.

"I understand. However, there are some things that God did not hide from us, but He hid them for us. What makes something a treasure is that it is either rare or hard to get to. Some of the greatest treasures of knowledge and understanding will only come with great perseverance. Anything that happens too fast or too easily is usually insignificant. I think some of your questions are important, and I will not presume to be able to answer them easily or quickly, but I will share with you what I have found in my own search.

"To keep from falling into another heresy, what seems partial or incomplete to us we must leave that way until He gives a clear revelation that we can confirm in the Scriptures. If we cannot verify a revelation in the Scriptures then we cannot accept it as doctrine. Prophecy or revelations are never given to establish doctrine, but only the Scriptures can do that. If you examine the roots of many cults and sects, you will almost always find a 'revelation' that cannot be verified by Scripture. If Jesus, who was the Word, would take His stand on 'it is written,' how much more do we need to do this?"

"Is your understanding of these issues established in the Scriptures?" Mary asked.

"Yes, but that does not mean you will see it. There is something else more basic required to understand the Scriptures."

"What is that?"

"You have to be willing to accept the conclusion and obey it, regardless of whether you like it or not. Jesus said, '*If any man is willing to do His will, he shall know of the teaching, whether it is of God, or whether I speak from*

*Myself.*" So to be able to understand the truth we must be willing to obey it.

"There was a dispute between Aquinas and Abelard about whether we need to understand in order to believe, or do we need to believe in order to understand. According to what Jesus said, we must not only believe, but be willing to obey Him in order to know whether His teachings were from God."

"That can be a challenge," the young Mary said.

"It is meant to be a challenge," I responded. "We have to see the Lord's glory with an unveiled face to be changed into His image. Our own prejudices, our good or bad experiences, can be veils that cause us to distort His teachings. Before we are trusted with the ultimate truth we must settle in our hearts that He is God, He is the Creator, and has the right to do what He wants with His creation. That is basic, but to trust Him we must also establish that He is just and will never do anything unjust."

"So you don't think He would condemn to eternal damnation those who never had a chance to hear and respond to the gospel?" the young Mary said quite loudly.

"I know that our God would never do anything unjust. Neither do I think we have to distort our concept of justice to make it fit what He does. Everything He does and everything that He will allow in His kingdom will be both righteous and just because '*Righteousness and justice are the foundation of His throne*' or His authority. You can count on this," I offered. You can also count on His love for all men."

That is when I saw Elijah again, standing nearby. I was obviously facing the questions he had warned me about. I looked around at the group. I knew that some might not make it past this point if they were not satisfied with the answers to some of these questions. Some would only make it past this point because of what I was about to say to them. I do not remember ever feeling this kind of pressure while feeling this inadequate. I prayed earnestly in my heart for the help of the Holy Spirit.

"Amen," I heard Elijah say. As I looked up, I was surprised to see him walking toward us.

That is when a loud noise came from the direction of the path. Two of the watchmen came running into the open, breathing hard while trying to yell:

"There's a lion after us!"

Elijah turned and swiftly grabbed both of the watchmen, saying, "Why are you running? There's a much bigger lion in you!"

Then he entered the woods walking, but resolutely moving toward the lion. The questions were no longer the most important issue for anyone.

"Let's go," I said, and we entered the path behind Elijah.

## CHAPTER SIX

# THE TEACHER

Neither Elijah nor the lion could be seen or heard. They seemed to have just vanished into the wilderness.

"It was the biggest lion I've ever seen," one of the watchmen said. "I can't believe Elijah would just go after it like he did."

"Did you hear what he said?" Mary asked.

"What did he say?" the watchman replied.

"That there is a bigger lion in us," Mary answered.

"What did he mean by that?" someone asked.

"But that lion was real!" the watchman declared.

"So is the lion in you," a familiar voice said.

Elijah was standing beside the path in front of us. He turned to the still shaken watchman, and continued:

"If you do not learn to face the lions, you will be running from them the rest of your life. If you do not chase them they will chase you far from your purpose, and you will die in this wilderness."

"But we need a big gun to face a lion like that," the watchman protested.

"You have weapons that are more powerful than guns. As I said, 'The Lion that is in you is greater.' If you see the Lion who lives in you, you will not be afraid of any other lion or anything else. You will not make it through this place without seeing the One who lives in you," Elijah countered.

"I helped you this time. Don't count on me being this close to you the next time they attack. They will be back, and they will keep coming back until you have made them more afraid of you than you are of them."

Everyone stood considering what Elijah said. The entire wilderness experience had taken on a much more serious air. Knowing the doctrine of Christ in us was not enough; we would have to live by the reality that He is in us. Seeing the Lord and abiding in Him was no longer just an option, but it would mean life or death.

After a few minutes, Mary walked up to Elijah and looking him directly in the eyes asked,

"Are you the real Elijah?"

"What does your heart tell you?" he replied.

After a minute, Mary answered with less boldness, "You really are Elijah. I'm sorry, but it's just hard to believe that we would be so special to have you come to help us."

"Why do you think it is so special to have me help you?" Elijah countered, looking at her just as resolutely. "Is not having the Holy Spirit living in you as your Helper even greater? I was given this honor to represent all of the prophets and righteous ones who helped to prepare the way for the Lord, but you have One greater than all of us with you always. Seeing the One who lives in you is much greater than seeing me. You must not be so distracted by those who bring you the words of the Lord that you do not see the Word Himself and follow Him.

"Even so, you are special. These are special times, and those who have been chosen to live in them are special. All who have walked this path are special, but to walk it in these times is one of the greatest honors there will ever be."

"Did you come because you knew the lion was going to attack us?" someone else asked.

"No. I came because of the questions you were asking."

"Are those questions wrong?" Mary asked with a humility I had not seen in her before.

"No. They are important just as your leader said to you. It is important that you get answers to the deepest questions you have. Some of you will not make it through this place without having answers to your questions."

"It's still hard to believe that you would come to personally answer our questions, and would appear to us for that," Mary said softly.

"I did not come to answer your questions, and there is something more important than having me come," Elijah said. "I was sent by the King. It is more important that the Lord cares about your questions."

Then Elijah motioned for us to begin walking, saying, "It is important for you to make as much progress as you can when you have light. You must keep moving."

As we walked past him I turned to look, but he had already faded into the trees. We all walked in silence for a time. Some were deep in contemplation. Others were watching and listening for any sign of lions. After more than an hour, Mary came up to me.

"Elijah will come back to answer our questions, won't he?"

"He may come back, but not to answer your questions," I replied.

"But I thought he said he was sent by the King Himself to answer them?"

"Remember the verse where the Lord said to *'be careful how you hear.'* Elijah said he came because of your questions, but he did not say he came to answer them. He came to convey to me how important they are and to tell me that I had the answers. Remember that I said to you that Elijah did not even know what the questions were. He was curious about them too."

"I'm sorry. I know you said this. It's strange to me that after being caught up to and dwelling in heaven all of this time he wouldn't have the answers to every question we could have," Mary surmised.

"He might know the answers, if he knew the questions. Elijah is one of the greatest prophets of all time, but he is not God, so he is not omniscient or omnipresent. He has limitations too."

"We assume a lot, don't we?" Mary confided. "I just assumed that everyone who had gone to heaven would know everything…."

"Like God? We do make many assumptions, don't we? The Scriptures do speak of how we will take on the divine nature, but after Jesus was resurrected and appeared to His disciples, He said that He had not yet been glorified. Of course He has now, but that does not mean that all of the saints who have gone before us have yet been glorified. There seems to be a distinction between being resurrected and being glorified. In Hebrews, it says that those who have gone before cannot be made complete, or perfect, without us. It could be that all are waiting for the last members of the body of Christ to take their place before they can receive their full reward or are glorified. And still, to be glorified may not mean that we instantly know everything. Maybe eternity is continual learning and exploring."

We walked in silence for a few minutes. Mary was deep in thought. She and William were remarkable people, but very different. I looked at the others, and wondered if they would all turn out to be so unique. I could see spending eternity just getting to know those who walked the earth and being endlessly fascinated. I was again thankful for having to come back and get this group, and I hoped to have the time to get to know them.

Mary then spoke up, "You have an interesting perspective, but to bring things a little closer to home, do you know what my questions are?" Mary continued.

"Elijah said that I could answer them because I had the same ones, so I do think I know what they are."

"And you have the answers?"

"I have answers. I spent years studying questions I could not get anyone else to answer to my satisfaction. When I began to search for the answers I felt that my research was guided by a special hand. I was being shown things that I felt I needed to know. I came to conclusions that satisfied me, but I'm not sure they will satisfy you.

"As I shared with the younger Mary, it is written that we see in part and know in part. I do not claim to have the whole answer to anything, but what I have found may help you. I also suspect that you will have to add your own conclusions to them. You have a part to add also.

"More important than the answers themselves could be the path to finding them so that you get them yourself. I just hope that I can help you find the path and the peace that comes from complete faith in our King being totally righteous and totally just."

"You said that you were shown the answers. How were you shown them?" the younger Mary asked, as she and others had begun to walk with us and listen.

"That may be the most important question of all," I replied. "My quest was for the answers, but when I found them I realized the trail that had led me to them was more valuable than the answers. This is the trail that can lead to all of the other answers."

"Can you explain this trail?" Mary asked.

"When I could not find a person with the answers, I took my questions to the Lord in prayer. He answered them in special and exciting ways. He became my Teacher, and He is better than any human teacher could ever be." I said. "This is why I think your questions are so important. Even more important than getting the answers is coming to know Him as your Teacher."

"Did He appear to you Himself or send someone like Elijah or an angel to teach you?" someone asked.

"No. I have seen the Lord, and I've seen angels, but none of those experiences were to answer my questions. I always thought that if I could see Him I would ask Him everything. But when He appeared to me I could not even think of a question. In fact, I was speechless and so full of the fear of the Lord that I could not imagine asking a question then, but that is another story.

"The way He became my Teacher was that after I prayed and asked Him to teach me about something, He would teach me in unique ways that I came to recognize as His ways. Someone might give me a book or a recorded message that would have the answer to a question, but I knew it was the Lord Himself giving it to me. At other times, I would feel compelled to watch a movie or television show, and it would have the answer to my question. Even though my answer may have been spoken by a character in the show I knew it was the Lord Himself answering my question. So I was not just hearing the words of the Lord, I learned to hear the Word Himself through whomever He chose to speak or by whatever means.

"Once I was sitting in an airport and prayed for the answer to a question, and a couple next to me began to talk. I could not help but hear their conversation, and I heard the answer to my question. There are no coincidences for those on the quest, but rather divine encounters. At other times, it was years before He answered a question, but it was still a divine encounter and always special."

"I think I've experienced a little of this, but never thought about it as the Lord being my Teacher," Mary offered.

"I'm sure you've experienced it. Most probably have. What we need to do is pursue this as the life of a disciple, which is to be taught by their Master.

"The relationship I built with my Teacher became more wonderful than the answers to my questions. I came to understand how the Lord has a special delight in teaching His people. This was the kind of fellowship He had with Adam in the Garden. I think it is the exploring, inquisitive nature of man that most touches His creative nature. He does not just endure our questions—He loves them.

"When in the pursuit of knowledge you begin to recognize His hand in teaching you, I call this a 'God trail.' It is like a great adventure. Again, God does not hide things from us, but He hides them for us. The answers I found were treasures, but the greatest treasure of all was the adventure and the relationship that I built with the Lord as my Teacher. I treasure some of the ways my questions were answered as much as I treasure the answers."

"I've had that happen too," someone in the group said, and many of the others agreed.

That was not only interesting for me to hear, but indicated to me that this really was a special group. In my many years of being in pursuit of God, I had found many who had experienced this, but not many who had learned that this was to be a main part of their life. As I surveyed the group, I could tell that they really understood this. I concluded that this was likely a factor for those who would find the path we were on. Only William seemed to be captivated by this as if it was a new thought, and of course, he was a new believer.

"Can you explain that a little more?" said William.

"Do you really think He wants to relate to everyone that way, not just those called to walk this path?" the younger Mary asked, obviously still thinking about her family.

"It is written that He has called us into fellowship with the Son, so He wants to have this kind of relationship with all of His people. It seems our failure to fulfill The Great Commission has robbed many of this. Our commission is to make disciples, not just converts. A disciple is a student. However, biblical discipleship is much more than being a student. A disciple is to have a single-minded purpose of learning from their master and becoming like their master. This should be the single most important devotion of our life, our first thought in the morning and our last thought before sleep."

"You would not have done well as the captain of our ship," someone remarked.

"I'm sure that's true, but it's interesting to me that you would say that. Why do you think that is so?" I asked.

"Out of the thousands on our ship, we are the only ones who would give any attention to trying to understand the times, the coming kingdom, or pursue the disciplines that lead to maturity. The more we did this the more skeptical the others became of us. Even the elders warned us about 'going too far'. What you are talking about is not popular."

"Well I guess it is a good thing that I never had the goal of being popular. My goal has been to know the Lord and be known by Him. I don't think there could be anything worse than having spent a life laboring for Him and then hear on that great Judgment Day that He never knew us."

"How could He not know us? I never understood that," the older Mary asked.

"The word 'know' in that verse is not the same one for having an acquaintance. It implies having an intimate knowledge of another such as a husband and wife would have of each other.

"Mary, what are some of your biggest questions?" I inquired.

"You know, I think the biggest question has already been answered," Mary said, as I noticed tears running down her cheeks. "To know that He cares enough to send Elijah just to tell you how important my questions are made me feel His love. All that you have said... I really want to know Him more than just have my questions answered. They're still important, but suddenly they are now a quest instead of a stumbling block for me.

"I have been so disappointed in people," Mary admitted. "Even notable men and women of God would get offended by my questions. All of them would tell me the same thing, 'Just trust in the Lord.' I want to, but I do have questions. Just knowing that He cares about my questions and wants to answer them gives me more trust than I've ever felt before. That helps me more than you could know."

"Do you want to ask any of your questions now?" I asked, stopping.

"No. I don't think so. The anxiety I had about my questions is gone. I still have the questions, but I'm okay to wait. Just knowing He cares about me like this is so wonderful I just want to enjoy this for a while. Can we wait?"

"Of course," I replied. "But I would like to say, it is one of the greatest blessings to have so many great teachers in our time. However, our biggest questions, the deepest issues of our heart, we should inquire of God rather than men. Although He will usually teach us through the teachers He has given to His people, He wants to be our Teacher. Only when we know Him as our Teacher will we be as strong as we need to be for what is before us. This is the Rock that He said He would build His church on— revelation that we receive straight from the Father. Of all the adventures we are going to experience, this is the best."

*"For they drank of that spiritual Rock that followed them, and that Rock was Christ."*

## CHAPTER SEVEN

# THE LIFE

I knew we needed to get moving to try to cover some ground before dark, but the peace of God was so present, and everyone seemed deep in communion with Him. I decided this was more important, and it was not a bad place to camp, so I relaxed.

As I sat surveying the group, I could not help but be inspired. They had such passion, such depth. They were alive, not just existing the way so many were. Before, I had entered the wilderness alone because I could not find any who would go with me. Everyone was so focused on the things of this world that they had little interest in going to the mountain I described. I was obviously looking in the wrong place. Who would have thought that such a group as this would have been on that luxury ship?

These had built a strong fellowship around their vision. Then they acted on it, not being content to just talk or dream. I was so thankful to be with them.

I turned to see Elijah sitting next to me. As if reading my thoughts, he began:

"In these times it is rare to find Christians who are interested in learning anything that is not about them personally, their benefits, how to prosper, etc. It can be important to know these things, but few are maturing

91

beyond this. Self-focus and self-centeredness are the nature of the immature. It is hard to find those who care about the deeper things of the Lord. Of those who do care, few are able to resist worldly distractions to actually pursue this knowledge and a relationship with the Lord—to be taught by Him. Those who do will pursue the city He is building."

"Thank you again for bringing me back to help this group," I said. "They've given me hope again."

"You had to come back for them. You were close to falling to what caused me to stumble at the end of my sojourn," Elijah reminded me. "I thought I was the only faithful one left. There are always more."

"Is the Lord going to appear to us here?" someone asked, as they saw Elijah sitting next to me.

"He is in your midst now," the prophet replied. "When the eyes of your heart are opened you will see Him. Do not be concerned about seeing Him with your natural eyes. It is more important that you see with your spiritual eyes. This journey will help to open your eyes so you can see."

I was impressed how Elijah had said this to inspire, not to condescend. I could feel the affection in him growing for this group. I began to think that he could have been a very good pastor, when he turned to me, raised one eyebrow, and looked at me as if he knew something I didn't. I started to ask him what he was thinking when he turned back to the people who were gathering in front of us and began to speak to them.

"You are going to the mountain of the Lord—that is, His kingdom, but the kingdom is already in your midst. The kingdom is His domain. As you learn to live in His domain you will be more at home there than you have ever been anywhere. When you get to the mountain you will be coming home. That's because the kingdom is where the King is, and He is your home just as you are His."

I thought about how many times I had taught this, maybe even using the same words, but listening to Elijah share them was like me hearing them for the first time. I was as captivated as anyone. His words did not just teach you how to know the Lord, but they made you want to know Him more than anything else. When I looked up, he was looking at me as if he was listening to my thoughts again.

"Please share what you are thinking," Elijah said to me.

"I was thinking about how many times I have said what you just said. But when you said it, there was a life and power that compelled and drew you to pursue the Lord," I answered.

"Do you know why?" Elijah asked.

"I think it is because you are sharing words that are Spirit and life, because they are your life," I answered.

"Truth that is life is truth that is lived," he continued. "As you live what you learn, your words will have the power of life. You will not just teach the truth, but you will impart a love for the truth when it is your life.

"When the Baptist preached he drew all Judea out to him. They did not come to see him because of how he dressed, or because he used powerful and beautiful words. They did not come out to him because of who he was, because they did not know who he was. They came because of the anointing. He had words of life that would lead to the path of life, the same path you are now on. You are not here just to learn the truth, but to live the truth.

Then your words will do the same as John's—compel men to follow the Lord. This is how you must prepare the way for the Lord.

"When the Lord told His disciples about the signs of the end of the age, He said, '*Woe to those who nurse babes in those days.*' He was speaking literally, but as you have interpreted this as 'Woe to those who keep their people in immaturity,' this is also true. They are still immature when they only want to learn things that are about themselves. There is a lot of teaching today that keeps people self-centered rather than Christ-centered. This keeps them in immaturity.

"You must all come to know the Teacher's voice, regardless of how He speaks or who He speaks through. Obviously, many of you have, at least, begun to learn this. But this is just the beginning. You must also learn to obey Him. To obey Him almost always requires risk and the disregard for self-interest.

"You would not be here if you were not learning this, but more than seeking to die to your own interests, you must seek the interests of Christ. Then your own selfish interests will begin to seem as small and petty as they are."

Elijah abruptly stood up, walked into the bush, and was quickly out of sight. We were all looking in the direction he had gone when a terrible roar came from the trees nearby, sending the entire group scurrying together, and screaming.

"Where did that come from?" I asked.

They all pointed in the same direction.

"Then turn and face it. There is nowhere to run."

The group had hardly finished turning in the direction of the roar when a massive black lion leapt into the clearing nearby. It scanned the group as if choosing a victim. Then it locked eyes with me. It started to crouch as if it were about to pounce when Mary stepped right in front of it, causing the big cat to almost fall backward in surprise. A moment later it vanished into the trees.

A terrible fear had gripped me when the lion locked eyes with me. I could still hardly move when I felt a hand on my shoulder. It was Elijah. The group was busy congratulating Mary, who was visibly shaken too. After a few minutes, they turned to see Elijah standing with me and quieted down. He began:

> "Mary just saved you from a great tragedy. That lion was here to kill and had a person in mind. As I said, if you face the lion and resist it, then it will flee from you. Never turn your back to the lion or to any attack. You all did well to at least face it. Mary, you can expect to be its next target. But you did well, and you do not need to fear being its target. When you face the lion he will see the Lion that lives in you."

I was thinking of how I would likely have been devoured by the lion if it had not been for Mary and wondered why it had not attacked me when I had gone through this wilderness alone. Elijah, who had just stood by and watched the entire event, turned to me and said:

> "There could be only two reasons why the lions did not attack you when you were alone. Either you somehow slipped past them unnoticed because they did not expect anyone to come through here alone, or because they saw you but did not think you had a chance of making it alone, so they did not bother. They will not likely make that mistake again. For them to so brazenly attack you in a group

like this is a sign of their desperation. This is a good thing. They are threatened by you, as they should be. From now on, they will be looking for any opening to attack."

"What kind of opening?" someone asked.

"The biggest opening the lions have is a division among you. Any who begin to separate from the group will be easy prey. They will not waste any time attacking stragglers or those who go off on their own," Elijah answered.

"Am I endangering this group by being with them?" I asked Elijah quietly, thinking about how this lion was obviously after me personally.

"They would be in greater danger without you," he answered. "Now, continue with what you were doing before the attack. You must deal with attacks, but do not let them sidetrack you. If the lions cannot devour someone, then they still win if they can turn us from something important that we're engaged in. For them to have attacked right then, and so brazenly, you were doing something crucial."

"We were discussing knowing the Lord's voice and the cost of obeying His voice," the young Mary said. "We were also enjoying a wonderful presence of the Lord."

"The timing and manner of the enemy's attack is important to understand. It is the lion's nature to hide and stalk until there is an opening. It is most uncommon for one to attack openly as that one did. It was desperate, and it was desperate because what you were doing was such a threat," the prophet continued. "The three things you were doing are the greatest threats to the enemy, and they are like the chord of three strands that can bind you together so that your unity cannot be broken. This is what you must have to make it to the mountain."

"Knowing the voice of the Lord, obeying Him, and dwelling in His presence," William recounted.

"Seal these three things in your heart," Elijah replied. "Resolve each day to get to know His voice better, to do His will, and to abide in Him. These will keep you, and they will lead you to the kingdom."

"You came to sit with us, and then abruptly disappeared just before the attack. You knew it was coming, didn't you?" the older Mary stated.

"Yes."

"Why did you leave just before the attack?" Mary persisted.

"Because it would not have attacked while I was with you."

"So you left so that they could attack us?" Mary said in disbelief.

"Yes."

"Why?"

"So that you would learn all that you've just learned."

"But we could have been killed!"

"Every day you are on this path you are in danger of that. The enemy is constantly prowling around you seeking someone to devour. You have to learn this, or you will not make it," Elijah replied.

"Some of you are now thinking about the safety of the luxury ship, even longing for it. Soon you will learn that there is even less safety on that ship than there is here. You are in the will of the Lord, and there is no safer place than being in His will. The Lion who is with you is much greater than those who are seeking to devour you. You must see the Lion who is in you, and you must, above all things, follow Him. You must not fear the lions that are seeking to destroy you, but you must resolve to make them fear you because of the One you abide in. That is the only safe place you can be."

"What did you mean that we would soon learn that the ship was not as safe as being here?" the young Mary asked.

"Everything that can be shaken is being shaken. Only the kingdom cannot be shaken. Those who are not in pursuit of the kingdom will be in increasing danger every day. Right now you are in the safest place you could be in this world," Elijah responded.

"Did something happen to the ship?" the young Mary asked again, even more resolutely.

"I can tell you this, Mary. You have found favor in the sight of the Lord, and He has shown mercy to your parents and to your loved ones on the ship," and with that Elijah slipped into the growing darkness of the forest.

We quickly set up camp by the stream. After drinking, posting the watchmen, and building a fire, we settled into a large circle to continue the discussion we were having when the attack came. I began:

"Even though we may not have covered much physical ground, I think we probably made more progress through this wilderness today than any other day yet. I would like to gather together each morning to review how we must pursue these three things and then again in the evening to recount how we have learned or grown in them.

"As we were discussing, any truth revealed by the Lord is a great treasure. Any story about a treasure hunt is filled with danger and suspense, so it seems we are in one of these now. We are actually on the greatest adventure and the greatest treasure hunt there can be in this life. I have not known you long, but already I think I have been privileged to be on this adventure with some of the greatest adventurers I've ever known."

"I've been in some meetings before that had a worldwide impact," William interjected. "In light of what we're experiencing here, those days seem petty and insignificant. I've never learned as many profound lessons in one day as I have this day."

"It's intensely wonderful and intensely scary at the same time. You were serious when you said that we should count every day as if it could be our last because it could. I thought you were being dramatic, but I'm sure I'll be taking everything you say more seriously now," another one said.

"Yes, but I'd rather not perish in this wilderness. I want to see the mountain. If I die, I'd rather die in battle there, so let's learn these three lessons and get through this place," another one countered.

"The first generation that left Egypt all perished in the wilderness. Their account is written for us so that the same does not have to happen to us. This journey is meant to be hard, and it is meant to be dangerous to prepare us for what we are called to, but we are not called to perish here.

We must know the Lord, know His voice, and obey Him in all things in order to make it. We must stay so close to Him that He is never out of our sight. We must learn to abide in the manifest presence of the Lord. If we ever lose that, we must stop and find Him. His presence is even more vital to us than this water," another added.

"That is why He allows those lions to roam here. They are for our sake—they drive us to the Lord," the older Mary said. "I have never felt Him like I have here, even like I do right now."

"I think we can learn in one day here what may have taken years to learn on that ship," William added.

"The whole world depends on Him for life," another one added. *'In Him we live and move and have our being,'* and here that is made real to us. We can't make it a single day without Him. We are here to learn this. The whole world is about to learn this, and we will be sent to the world with that message. This is the gospel of the kingdom that must be preached throughout the world. This message will not go forth in just words, but in power, the power of those who live it."

All I could think about was how much I loved my job.

## CHAPTER EIGHT

# THE CHALLENGE

After we all drank from the stream, we sat in a large semicircle to pray and for a short teaching in order to review all that we had been taught that day. There was much to process, but after the exhilaration of the day, we were emotionally exhausted. Even so, the living water quickened us so that the prayers were passionate, as was the discussion after the short teaching. I finished with a review of our three main purposes for each day:

- Knowing the voice of the Lord
- Obeying Him
- Dwelling in His presence

The next morning we drank and again sat to pray together and review our purpose for the day. We reviewed our three main purposes and challenged the group how we might make the most of our day, even if we had no lion attack, no visit from Elijah, or no other drama. The Lord's presence was very real. It was hard not to just want to sit there all day, but we began walking down the path.

We had not gone far when I found myself in a small group composed of both Marys, William, Mark, and a couple of others. William began the discussion:

"The knowledge of His ways is more valuable than any earthly treasure. We all agree on that. If that had not been clear before, yesterday fully established that. We have only been on this journey a few days but a pattern is developing. We discuss a principle or truth and then experience it's application. Can we expect this every day now?"

"If we abide in the Lord, this is one of the ways He teaches us," I answered. "He is the Way, the Truth, and the Life. For a truth to become life, it must be applied to our life. The Word says that the ways of the righteous are ordered by the Lord. He does order our steps to help turn what He is teaching us into life.

"We are promised in His Word that all who seek, find, and all who ask, receive. A more accurate translation would be that all who keep seeking find, and all who keep asking receive. The quest for these treasures of the knowledge of His ways is one of the greatest adventures you can know in this life, to a large degree because He adds to it the experience of the truth."

"If He wants all to be saved and come to the knowledge of the truth, and for all of us to know Him, why does He make it so hard?" the younger Mary asked.

"Only those who care enough to continue the pursuit of these treasures will find them. Those who care that much for them will likely be careful enough to handle them rightly. It is like any earthly fortune. Those who do not have the experience of building a fortune will not have the wisdom to keep it. Those who do not have the experience of searching out His treasures of wisdom and knowledge will not care enough to keep them or live them. Even so, the greatest treasure of all will be the fellowship we have with Him when He becomes our Teacher."

"When you were spending those years of research and study you spoke of, did you only read or listen to messages that you felt He had put in your hand?" the older Mary asked.

"No. I read and studied many things. I put the highest priority on any book or material I felt that He had specifically put in my hands, but only a small percentage of what I studied would I put in the category of knowing that it had been given to me directly by the Lord. They would often get me going on a trail, but I followed the trail with my own pursuit and research," I answered.

"Again, He is called 'the Helper' who was sent to be our Guide, not 'the Doer.' Once I got on a trail I would feel His guidance if I started to drift from it, and He would correct me and help me get back on the right track. I also learned that as Jesus said of Himself, He is gentle and humble of heart. He is gentle in the way He guides us. For this reason, we must stay sensitive to recognize His guidance and even His correction. He may use dramatic ways to get our attention as we learned yesterday with the lion, but that tends to be the exception, not the rule.

"I was taught when I was a new believer that He gave us the desires of our hearts. The things we desired in our innermost being were the things He was calling us to do. When I did not have a specific leading to study something or a book or message that I felt He had given to me, I followed my heart in my studies. It seemed to always pay off."

"Were there others like this that you had fellowship with?" one of those I did not know well asked.

"What is your name?" I inquired of the elderly lady.

"My name is Judy."

"Judy, that is a good question. There were a few that I had fellowship with around these things. They were rare but they were rich in substance. I thought some of our conversations were as revelatory as many books I had read. Sometimes I would ask the Lord a number of questions before meeting with these friends, and in our meeting, my questions would get answered, sometimes even in sequence. They may not even know the Lord was using them this way, but that made it even better. As close as we were drawn to one another, we were being drawn even closer to the Lord. I knew that He was my Teacher.

"However, just to meet someone with the same zeal for understanding was like finding an even greater treasure. The fellowship we had around these things was my first real taste of *koinonia*."

"Can you tell us a little more about yourself?" Judy asked.

"I think you deserve to know more about me since you have me here for at least a while," I began. "I had been an agnostic before coming to know that God was real. From the time I learned to read, I had a hunger to read everything I could get my hands on. I developed a love for knowledge. I wanted to know about everything, and had many interests, but I began to think that the greatest discovery anyone could ever make would be to know God. At the time, like most people, I was confused by religion, but I thought that if I could ever learn who the real God was I would spend the rest of my life getting to know Him. What could possibly be more important than that?

"Then I had a supernatural conversion experience that left me with no doubt that God is real and that Jesus is the Son of God and everything He said He was in the Scriptures. This was the greatest day of my life. I knew I had found the greatest treasure of knowledge anyone could ever find. I have been in constant awe and fascination with Him ever since. I cannot imagine life being more wonderful than getting to know Him and serving Him.

"It is written that '*God is Love*,' and I learned that you could not learn anything about Him without loving Him more. That compels you to learn more about Him so that you get caught up in an ever tightening and ascending life spiral that gets stronger and stronger. I call this 'the great addiction' that every other addiction is a counterfeit of. There is nothing that will ever satisfy the human soul like knowing God. Once you start to know Him, you just cannot get to know Him enough."

"To this I will attest," said Elijah who had joined our company without being noticed. "I have seen the glories of earth and heaven. The glories of heaven overshadow the greatest glories of earth more than can be conveyed, but the glory of God overshadows the glory of heaven even more so.

"I have sat in the great councils of heaven. The greatest of all marvels is how the Lord shares His glory with men, and how He intends to dwell on the earth among men. His love for man is more than anyone has yet comprehended. To know this is the greatest knowledge of all; this is the greatest treasure of all. The highest pursuit of all is to know Him."

We were all still pondering what Elijah had said. There was a long silence, but it was not awkward—it was holy. The presence of the Lord was so great that we just wanted to enjoy Him. After a long time, Mark spoke:

"The Lord built His first dwelling place among men in the wilderness with the children of Israel. It is here that He is building His dwelling place among us."

"Why did He just come upon us so strongly like that, here and now?" someone asked.

"Because we were talking about His love," the older Mary answered. "The real revelation was not in the words, but in what we felt—His love for us. He is with us. He loves us."

"He is with us all the time, we know, but it is so different when He comes upon us like this," someone else chimed in.

"This is His manifest presence," someone added. "He is with us all the time, but He does not always manifest Himself like this. Being with Him in His presence is like nothing else. This is what we were made for—to dwell with Him, to know His special fellowship."

We had to stop. It just was not possible to keep walking. The rest of the group gathered around, and we prayed and worshipped for a long time. No one wanted to leave. Many tears flowed. Then there was laughter. No jokes, just joy. We all seemed to know at the same time that we needed to start walking again. We all just got up and started.

"Do you feel rejuvenated?" William asked. "That was even better than the living water. I don't know if I have ever felt this good."

"'He is a quickening Spirit who will quicken our mortal bodies'," someone quoted.

"That was what King David called 'the sweet fellow-ship' they experienced in the house of the Lord," another chimed in. "There is nothing else like it. That is why David had to have the Ark with him in Jerusalem."

As we were basking in what we had just experienced, I looked around at the group and could not help but think of how much more wonderful it was to go through the wilderness with them. For this, I could be content to stay in the wilderness. The presence of the Lord is more wonderful than anything. I had not experienced anything like this when I went through this same place alone. I loved them all. I looked at the ones I had not even met yet, and I loved them and could not wait to get to know them.

"You are known to be a historian, especially with church history. What led you to study these?" someone asked me. "Did you read much about experiences like this with others?"

"I'll answer the last question first," I began. "Yes, some did write about their experiences with the manifest presence of the Lord. Those who experienced it described it differently in some ways, but there was a common thread. The result was always the same: an insatiable desire to be close to the Lord and *koinonia* fellowship with all who experienced it together, just as we are experiencing now.

"You could tell a difference in the writings of those who had experienced this. Their message was far more than just doctrine and principles. There was a life on it that made you not want to put the book down. I feel for all who sit for years under teaching and preaching, but never experience the Lord Himself. That is too common in our times, but I think it has been common since the first century. Ecclesia, the structure and government of the church, is a terrible thing without the *koinonia*—the fellowship with the Lord and His people we are called to have.

"As to your first question about what led me to study history, especially church history, I was given instructions to do so. I was told that is where some of the greatest treasures of wisdom and knowledge are found. It is true.

"The Bible is basically a history book. It's mostly about God's dealings with men and how He has accomplished His purposes through them in the past. History comes from the words His and story. My purpose for studying history was to see His works in it, and by this, to know His ways better. However, the first two years of studying church history were probably the driest times I've ever spent reading. I did not realize that I was building a foundation of general knowledge that was necessary for the great revelations that were to come. Without that foundation some of the greatest treasures I found would not have even made sense to me, and I would have likely discarded them. You must go through a wilderness to get to the Promised Land, and that wilderness is usually the exact opposite of what you've been promised. My wilderness lasted about two years in regard to my study of history, but since then it has been a most wonderful promised land."

"What was the single most important thing you learned from church history?" Mary asked.

"Without question it would be God's relentless pursuit of man and His unimaginable patience and love for man, even though He is constantly rejected or ignored by man. It's the most painful love story ever written, and it is not over. He is in relentless pursuit of a bride, but, to date she seems to have little or no time for Him. So far, it is the greatest of all tragedies, but we know it will have the most wonderful of all endings. He will have the bride that He is so worthy of."

"You said this as if you felt His pain. I could feel it too when you were sharing it," Mary said.

"There is a lot of suffering on earth, and it is right to have compassion for it," I continued. "But I think it is even more important to know the suffering of the Lord. His suffering did not end on the cross. He still intercedes for us because He still feels for our suffering, and it hurts Him. However, I don't think this will end until we see and are touched by His suffering and devote ourselves to seeing the bride that He is so worthy of make herself ready for Him, and they are united. Then, the end of all suffering can come, and the new age in which His kingdom comes will begin.

"Spiritual maturity begins when we stop being self-focused and begin to focus on serving the Lord and helping others. Advancement in the kingdom comes by becoming greater servants of others. We were created for His pleasure, and nothing will ever satisfy our own souls like fulfilling this purpose. To spend a lifetime just to bring Him joy for a single moment would be a life well lived, but we can bring Him joy every day. What do we have to do that is more important than that?"

We walked on in silence for a time. I looked around at the rest of the group. All but a few were now in small groups. Most were talking as they walked, some laughing, others seemingly in deep discussions. There were a few individuals walking alone, but they seemed to want this, caught up in their own thoughts or praying. It was a special time, no trauma or drama yet. It seemed to be just what we needed after the intensity of the day before. The presence of the Lord was so strong that I felt like we were children out on a walk with our Father. It was a revelation that such a desolate place could be so wonderful.

Soon I could tell that Mary had more questions she wanted to ask, so I encouraged her to:

"What is on your mind?" I began.

"What you shared about your lessons from history was profound. I never want to forget it. Can you share anything else? I don't think we will have as much time to study as you did, and I want to learn all I can while we have the chance," she began.

"You're a practical person, so I will share with you what I think is the most practical lesson I learned from studying history: The saying is true that 'those who do not know history are doomed to repeat it.' The repetitious cycles of history are tragic. Mankind has made impressive progress in many ways, but in some of the most basic, the most important issues of all, we do not seem to have learned much. We keep repeating the same mistakes.

"The church has been just as guilty of this as the rest of the world. Every spiritual generation tends to make the same mistakes as the previous generations. Of course, any historian or student of history will see this, and some have offered solutions, but to date, we have not escaped from this terrible downward spiral. This is the cause of the worst human tragedies, and why they are repeated over and over."

"That is the most important lesson?" William inquired. "It's become such a cheap cliché that everyone repeats."

"You're right. Everyone says it, and I think most really believe it, but they keep doing it," I answered.

"Why do you think this is?" someone else asked.

"It's a combination of things, but I think the most prevailing reason is pride. The core of this pride causes every generation to think that they are better than the last one. We tend to think we are smarter, wiser, and definitely not like our parents, and this keeps us in the trap. As we grow older, we become just like our parents, or out of a reaction to our parents and trying to be different from them, we become even more shallow shells of who we could be. Reactions to the problems of our parents, or anyone else, will not get us free of this trap. Only repentance, and the humility that would enable us to be teachable, will get us free.

"The Lord gave us the answer to this dilemma when He gave the law to Moses and commanded us to honor our fathers and mothers. He did not say honor the great ones, or even just the good ones, but whatever parents we got. I think if our mindset was to honor those who have gone before us instead of disregarding them, we could even learn so much from the bad ones that our progress could be multiplied.

"Alex Haley once said that when an old person dies it's like a library burning down. That our elders are not listened to, that we do not try to learn all that we can from those who have been this way before, is one of our greatest mistakes, and the reason why we repeat the great mistakes of history over and over.

"The great teachings and great truths can become common, but it is rare to find anyone who has been changed by the truth. Multitudes can quote the great teachings of the faith, but it is rare to find those who are living them. I think humility must be mixed with the truth in order for it to change us.

"God commanded Israel to repeat their history every year. This was not to get them to live in the past, yet we cannot deal with the present or the future as we should if we forget the lessons of the past. Not respecting the past enough to study it is probably the main cause that so many empires have risen, through all that it takes to build such a thing, only to quickly disintegrate for the lack of a simple, basic, understanding.

"The command to honor our fathers and mothers is the only commandment with a promise. It is found in both the Old and New Testaments. The promise is that it will go well with us, and we will live long in the land that the Lord has given us. The short-lived empires, businesses, or families are often so unnecessary. To honor our fathers and mothers requires much more than just knowing their stories, it is continuing with a respect for their teachings."

"How can we get that honor?" someone asked.

"It is much easier to teach on the grace of God than to walk in it. It is all grace, but only those who pursue Him find His grace. We must care enough about this command of the Lord to pursue what it means to honor our fathers and mothers. I don't think there is a certain formula for it. We have to care enough to seek to understand it and then to do it.

"It can begin with caring enough to know their story and to hear what they have to say. We have much teaching on faith, but the Word says that it takes faith and patience to inherit the promises. I think the patience part often gets left out. It takes great patience to study history or to listen to our elders, but those who do are rewarded.

"One of the great revelations of God in history is His seemingly infinite love for, and patience with, man. We are ever learning but not coming to the knowledge of the truth. Even so, He sends His witnesses to every generation and tries to help us. Every generation resists those who are sent to them, and then they stumble over the same stumbling blocks as the previous generations, but He keeps reaching out to man. Even the few who honor His witnesses seldom really do what they say. Yet the Lord has never given up on us. He remains faithful even when we are so unfaithful."

"Do you see any hope for our generation?" the younger Mary asked.

"Yes. I see great hope. Your generation could be the one that breaks the cycle, fulfills its purpose, and truly prepares the way for the coming of the kingdom," I responded.

"Before I give the main reason for this hope, please bear with me to share a couple of other principles I've learned. What may at first discourage us can lead to an even greater, more substantial hope. The true hope that will never disappoint us often has to begin with losing our hope in men, but that is when we can put our hope in the only One who is worthy of our trust—the Lord. Our hope cannot be in people, even God's people, but in Him.

"What has kept me going and believing in the ultimate glorious victory of the church is that my trust is in God to bring this to pass, not people. To be disillusioned means to lose your illusions. That is a good thing, but then we must replace the illusions with faith. True faith is always centered on God, not men.

"True faith cannot be based on anything but truth. Part of the truth is to see our true condition, but even more importantly, to see God's heart and purposes for us. Israel went through repetitious cycles of: trusting Him and seeing His victory; forgetting Him and falling into apostasy; falling into bondage; crying out to Him for deliverance, and He would deliver them, over and over. The church has done the same thing throughout history.

"Through all of this, God has never lost His patience or His hope in us, because He is not really trusting in us as much as He is in His Holy Spirit to bring this to pass. There will be a generation that breaks this downward cycle we have been trapped in, and your generation is showing signs that it could be the one.

"We can be sure that the one that does break out of this terrible trap will be a generation that learns to honor their fathers and mothers. They will learn the lessons without having to repeat past mistakes, because they will resist the delusion that they are so much smarter or better than previous generations. That generation will break through and possess the Promised Land.

"One of the things that gives me hope in your generation is the profound arrogance that is now gripping it, and the way that pride and rebellion is being glorified," I said.

"How would that give you hope? Isn't that the opposite of what we need to be embracing?" Mary almost blurted out.

"Yes, it is, and that is the point. A main factor about the times is that the end of the age is the harvest. A main factor about the harvest is that all of the seeds that have been sown are coming to maturity, both the good ones and the evil ones. The pride and arrogance of man seems to be coming to full maturity in your generation, but we can also know by this that the good seeds will mature too.

"When the Lord spoke about the end of the age, He said that He would send His angels to gather out of His kingdom all of the stumbling blocks. The tares will be reaped first, and that will leave the wheat.

"True sojourners do not follow the masses, but always move in the opposite spirit of this world. The pride and arrogance of man has reached the levels that were prophesied for the end of this age. It cannot get much worse, so those who overcome this darkness will be some of the strongest ever. Those who overcome pride will be some of the most humble and, therefore, the most teachable and wise of all time.

"*'Where sin abounds grace does that much more abound.'* God gives His grace to the humble, and God's grace is the most valuable of all treasures. There is nothing that can stop God's grace, and there is nothing that cannot be accomplished with God's grace. We are getting close to the time when the humble will inherit the earth. They will do this because they walk in God's grace. Therefore, the greatest in the kingdom are the most humble. Your generation will produce some of the greatest in the kingdom because they will be some of the most humble."

## CHAPTER NINE

# THE LEADER

As we were walking, William drew me aside so that we would be far enough from the others that no one would hear us. Something was bothering him. He seemed compelled to talk about it as we walked in the morning sun.

"I've been watching how you handle this group," William began. "This is a unique situation, and I am interested in understanding your methods."

"I appreciate your interest, and I would very much like to hear your insights," I replied.

"I was concerned that you have been too candid about your own failures and weaknesses. The group needs to trust you, and I'm not sure this is helping. However, I have to admit I could tell that this did cause some to trust you even more, maybe because of your transparency. Is that what you were trying to achieve?"

"It may have worked out that way, but I did not do it for that reason," I replied. "My reason for being transparent is because I was given a job to do—to get this group through this wilderness. They will only make it by their faith in God, not me. I know there is a certain trust they must have in me as God's provision for them at this time, but my goal is to get them to the place where they do not need me. I want to get them there as fast as I can. I want them to make it, even if I do not make it."

"That is a remarkably selfless way to think," William responded.

"It may not be as selfless as it seems," I explained. "If I fail but they succeed, then I have still accomplished something, and my efforts will not have been in vain. I have had great teachers myself. Some of them finished well, and some did not, but I know that the fruit that I bear will still go to their account because of all that they invested in me. So I want to accomplish all that I can for their sakes as well, especially the ones whose lives seemingly ended in failure. They can still succeed through me if I do.

"I am grateful for those who sowed into my life even if they did not finish well, but I confess that I am also doing this for selfish reasons. As I said earlier, the only commandment with a promise is to honor our fathers and mothers. The promise is that it may go well with us, and we would have longevity. I want to honor them because I do care for them, but also because I have learned the great benefit we receive for doing this."

"Your candor is appreciated but, again, I wonder if it is helpful to be so transparent with everyone," William replied.

"You may be right. I might not be so candid with immature or unstable ones, but these are different. I cannot treat these as followers, but as co-laborers. Any one of these could mature here much faster than I have and deserve this position of leadership more than me. If so, I want to make that transition as smoothly and as quickly as possible."

"I have never heard any leader talk like that," William replied.

"William, my goal here is not leadership. I did not ask for this position nor want it. This is an assignment that I am honored to have, but it is a duty. My purpose is to grow in Christ like everyone else here. Did He not lay down His life and give His leadership to others? I want to be the best leader that I can be for His sake and their sakes. My purpose is not to be the leader, but getting them through this wilderness. I will quickly defer to anyone that can do a better job at this than me with, of course, the approval of the One who is the Leader of us all. Sometimes the greatest leadership can be to know when to give up the leadership and follow.

"A long time ago, I was told that the leadership that would get us to our destination was modeled by geese. They fly in a V formation behind the leader, because it is about 30% easier to draft behind others than it is to be in the lead. Therefore, the leader will tire much faster than those behind. If the flock is to keep up its pace, getting as far as it can as quickly as it can, it must regularly change leaders. If my weariness begins to slow the whole group down, I will need to let someone else take over, at least for a while, until the same thing happens to them. I am already looking for who might be next so I can help prepare them for it."

"It makes great sense, but I have never heard anything like this before from anyone in leadership," William replied.

"Here things are different than in the world. To be a leader is a very shallow goal. Getting to the mountain with all who have been entrusted to us is the goal. I do not want to let anything, even my own place, eclipse that purpose."

"Are you thinking that I might be one of those called to lead for a time?" William asked.

"Yes." I replied.

"But I am a new believer, younger than any of the others here. Doesn't The Bible warn against giving leadership to new believers?"

"It does. I am mindful of that too. However, maturity in Christ is not just the result of the passage of time. It is much more the result of how we deal with the trials we are given. It is the result of being humble enough to be teachable, but even more than this, it is the result of getting close to the King and learning from Him.

"I have spent my life seeking to know the Teacher. He is the One who told me that to make it through this place I had to put the interests of all others above my own. The right answer to every crisis or problem is to put the interests of others first. In one sense you could say that I am doing this selfishly to get through this by putting their interests above mine. It is in their best interest to get to the place as fast as possible where they could make it without me if they needed to."

"I know selfishness and selfish ambition very well from my experience. With everyone I worked with, it was all about them. If this is what is driving you, then you are hiding it very well," William remarked.

"Again, thank you. It is encouraging for you to say that because I often feel like the most selfish person I know. I honestly do not know if I am just able to hide it well. Even so, I do know this: so many in these times gave their lives to Christ, but were then taught to follow people, movements, or certain doctrines, and were never led to Him.

At best, this always leads to disappointment and a shallow, frustrating life far from the abundant life they were promised. There is only one foundation that we can build upon, and that is Christ Himself. I really did not mean to share anything for the purpose of getting people to trust me more or less, but to turn them to the only One who will never fail them or disappoint them."

"I believe you're sincere in this, but I've just never seen this approach to leadership. I have not been in Christ for very long, and this is a very different approach than I have ever seen. Even on the ship, it was all about the leaders. They were mainly devoted to getting people to trust in them and follow them. I often felt the same kind of selfishness and self-centeredness that I felt in the political leaders I've served and just assumed that was normal. Even the visiting speakers all seemed to be doing the same thing, trying to get people to trust in them as God's man or woman of the hour. Is this the general practice of the church, or was their stream an exception?" William asked.

"My experience with that particular stream is limited, and I would not want to base my judgment on such a brief experience with them," I answered. "I have been to many streams and movements in the body of Christ, maybe even most of them. I have found treasures and strengths in all of them. Even so, I think the kind of leadership taught and demonstrated by the Lord and the early apostles is rarely found today. Those who demonstrate it all have very small ministries by today's standards. However, you can always tell a big difference in how much more mature and how much closer to the Lord those under their leadership are.

"The Apostle Paul lamented that the Corinthians would follow those who abused them and even slapped them in the face. But Paul came allowing his personal weaknesses to be seen, and they would not listen to him. Carnal people respond to carnal strength and carnal leadership. I'm afraid, by the biblical definition, the church, in general, is still carnal and immature. Do you think Paul should have changed his style of leadership so that the Corinthians would be more prone to listen to him?" I asked.

William did not immediately answer, but thought about this deeply before responding. This was impressive to me and so was his answer when he finally gave it:

"Christ Himself demonstrated the kind of leadership Paul did when He went to the cross. In Revelation 3, He stands outside the door of His own church knocking to see if any will open to Him. He does not force Himself on us. If we use any other kind of leadership than what He demonstrated, which is what I think Paul also used, we will not be leading people to Him," William said.

"There are not many who can see this," I responded. "Of those who see it not many actually walk in it. It is much easier to use carnal leadership to motivate carnal people than it is to help them mature. I pray that you will walk in the way of this great insight that you already have.

"Our goal must not be to just get people to do the right thing, but to get them to follow the King and to do the right thing because it is in their hearts. You can teach a parrot to say the right thing and do the right thing, but it will not be in its heart. God is seeking to give us a new heart and a new mind so that we obey Him from a true heart, not just out of compulsion.

"I know the traps and diversions ahead of us. The further we get, the more just having truth will not be enough to keep us. We must have more than truth; we must have a love for the truth to make it. Only with this love for the truth will we choose the right path when there are options. Only by following our love for God and His people will we avoid the traps.

"The Truth is a person that we must love above all else. Only this love will keep us close to Him, and only by staying close to Him will we be able to make it. We must get so close to Him that we are following Him, not just principles."

"I think you are doing the right thing by being as transparent as you are," William admitted. "Now I see why Paul wrote that he would rather glory in his weaknesses. He wanted the Corinthians to trust in the grace of God, not him. There is a place for honoring our spiritual fathers and mothers, and Paul was their spiritual father, but he was not afraid to come in weakness and fear so that the grace of God could be even more evident. This compelled them to build their faith on God, not him. This is a very different kind of leadership."

"William, I have met very few who grasp the things that you already understand," I responded. "Life is all about Jesus. If we stay close to Him, we will be changed by Him. Then we will begin to see with His eyes, hear with His ears, and understand with His heart. The way to fulfilling our purpose is to follow Him. He is The Way. To lead them through this wilderness, I must lead them to Him. There is no other way. I will fail, and we will all fail, if we do not find Him and follow Him."

"Again, my experience in the faith is limited, but as this is the kind of leadership that both the Lord and His apostles taught and demonstrated, why do we not see more of this kind of leadership in the church?" William asked again.

"There are a number of reasons. One is that many have reduced The Great Commission to making converts instead of disciples. When our vision is so shallow, then we can only impart such shallowness to those we lead.

"We are told that the Holy Spirit searches the depths, even the depths of God. No follower of Christ who has the Holy Spirit should ever be shallow in anything, much less their knowledge of God and His ways. This shallowness always results in many spiritual shipwrecks, and I think the shepherds may end up taking a lot of responsibility for these."

"Another reason for this shallowness is that few of those who have gained much influence in the body of Christ today have been through this wilderness. Few are leading their people to the mountain," Elijah responded, who had been listening nearby without being noticed. He continued:

"The kind of leadership they are using will work for people who are selfishly just seeking blessings and abundance for themselves, but it does not lead them to the kingdom. Selfishness will get you killed on the path that leads to the kingdom. It is only by being willing to lose our lives for the King and His people that you will find true life and stay alive here. The blessings of the Lord are to be received and appreciated, but when they become your focus and purpose, you will not make it to the mountain of the Lord. Neither will you be prepared for the great battle that is coming.

"Please continue," he said, nodding to me.

"Some of the greatest leaders in church history may be alive in our time," I said, looking at Elijah to see if he would acknowledge this, which he did.

"I have known some of them and learned from them, but everything I have learned has led me to conclude that the first transitional ministry that led to the ministry of Christ—John the Baptist—is the greatest type of New Covenant ministry."

"What do you see in the Baptist that is such a type of New Covenant ministry?" Elijah asked.

"John's whole purpose was to prepare the people for the coming of the Lord. Then he directed them to follow the Lord even though it meant that they would leave him. He was willing to decrease as the Lord increased, because this meant that he had fulfilled his purpose. We are not here to build our authority in people. We're not here to make people our disciples, but to make them His disciples.

"John came in your spirit. The Lord acknowledged this after He saw you on the Mount of Transfiguration. He said that you came with John, but you were also 'coming.' It was prophesied by Malachi that you would come at the end of the age. What is it about you that those who prepare the way for the Lord must come in your spirit?" I asked.

Elijah smiled. He then looked up as if he was asking what to do with me, or how to handle this question. After a pause, he began his answer:

"Not everything about my life is a good model for the last-day ministry. These are still good lessons because some of the things that caused me to stumble will be a threat to the last-day ministry. One of these is the way I gave in to depression or arrogance when I began to think that I was

125

the only one with truth or who was faithful to the Lord. These are still the primary traps that capture those who walk in great power.

"Keeping this in mind, I was a model of the most powerful ministry that will ever walk the earth, the ministry that is being raised up at the end of this age. I had to confront the evil Jezebel who had taken over our nation and all of her false prophets and religions. The same spirit is taking over much of the world today and especially your nation. This evil is manifesting in your government just as Jezebel used Ahab. This is an ultimate evil, and those who are the Lord's in this time will have to stand up to it, just as the Baptist also did as a type. There is much for you to learn about this, to do it without being rebellious, but nevertheless, disarming the powers of this age. This is given for the last-day ministry to do.

"Next, I raised up many other prophets for the times. I also gave special attention to the one who was called to replace me, to do even more than I did and walk in more power than I did, Elisha. You must do the same.

"The next task may be the most difficult of all. You must pray for the judgments of God to come upon your nations when they are needed, just as I did.

"To do all of these things, you must always keep the interests of God above the interests of men. The Lord does prefer mercy over judgment, as we all should, but when mercy does not work, then His judgment is mercy. You must understand this, because to be His prophet in these times you must be in agreement with Him and His purposes at all times, even when it is time for judgment.

"Can you call for the judgment of God to come upon your nation? The whole world is about to experience the kinds of judgments that came upon Egypt, and for the same purpose—to set God's people free. The time for judgment is at hand, and this will begin with His own household. Can you be in agreement with Him for this?"

Then Elijah paused and seemed to be gauging our reaction to this before he continued. I was also watching William, who seemed to grasp it all.

"All of this you must do, but you also have the higher purpose. The Baptist had a higher purpose than I did because he was to point to the Lamb of God and compel people to follow Him. You have an even greater purpose than this. You must follow Him yourself. You must abide in Him. You must become like Him, and you must do the works that He did, while pointing to Him."

"Any one of these things would be more than enough for any person," William remarked.

"This is true," Elijah admitted. "That is why those who will do these things are a great company. I was almost alone, as was the Baptist, but we were standing before a single, small nation. You must prepare the whole world for the coming of the Lord and His kingdom. For this reason, there will be a great army of such messengers."

"Will they all go to the mountain on this path?" William asked.

"They must all go to the mountain by this path," Elijah acknowledged.

"There are not many of us on this path now. Are there many more coming after us?" William continued.

"There have not been many to walk this path yet, even throughout the church age, but there have been some on it at all times. More are coming. There will soon be more on this path than have ever walked it throughout the church age. Everyone who makes it to the mountain will go back and get others. There is a mighty army now being gathered.

"Every one of these is a messenger. They are being prepared to shake cities and nations with the power of the message they will be given. In time, they will capture the attention of the entire earth, and everyone on earth will marvel at them. These will be 'the mighty ones' that Enoch prophesied would come. They are alive now, and they are starting to find this path," Elijah concluded, and walked away.

William and I sat for a time reflecting on what we had just been told. Finally William spoke:

"I always wanted to be close to those whose decisions shaped our world. I built my life around that desire. When I achieved this, it was far from the satisfaction I expected. I now see that I was with the wrong people, because the power was never linked to a transcendent cause. Now I have that cause, and I can see how this little band we're with could impact the world more than any congress or president. They may not look like much now, but these really are the great ones, aren't they?"

"I'm still learning about them too," I said. "There could be prophets in this little group that eclipse anything that the prophets of old did, even Elijah. There could be last-day apostles here who transcend anything that has ever been accomplished to prepare the way for the King. What happened in the first century was the seed, but we are coming to the time of the harvest. We may have in our company some of the greatest men and women of God to ever walk the earth.

"It is interesting that it was always your desire to be around world changers. You were able to do this in the natural, and now you're about to do it with the spiritual. I think we are going to find this to be common here—the things we do in the natural reflect our spiritual calling," I said.

"Seeing Elijah is far more than I would have ever expected," William replied. "Now I am being allowed to foresee what is about to be released on the earth. I already see that there could be some right here who eclipse what Elijah did. I feel more privileged to be here than in the most important offices of the greatest earthly leaders. Following Christ has already been more wonderful than I ever dreamed, and I'm just starting out.

"Being in those earthly centers of power always left me feeling agitated and empty. I could not understand this until now. On this path with these simple ones, I feel a greatness I never felt with the earthly great. Here I am energized, fulfilled. I feel a strange peace. I have been greatly blessed by the Lord to now meet and travel with the truly great, those who are with us here.

"Now, I don't mean to be critical, but I need to know how the expression of Christianity here could be so different than what I experienced on the ship? With them, I felt more like I did with the worldly than I do here with these."

"I don't mean to be critical either, but I think leadership is a key to understanding this. The greatest leaders here will be the greatest followers of Christ. It all comes down to who we're following, the King or our own ambitions, which is still ambition, even if we're doing it in the name of the King."

## CHAPTER TEN

# THE SEEKERS

William and I walked on in silence for a while. We were both deep in our own thoughts. William seemed to not only understand all that we had discussed about leadership in the kingdom, but he had grasped it with an uncommon depth. He was an example of how when the Lord calls someone He prepares them for their purpose throughout their whole life.

I started to think about the remarkable people in this group, what I could do to help them, and how I was going to answer Mary's questions when she decided to ask them. A small group of people walking nearby obviously wanted to talk, so I motioned for them to join us.

"So you think the great treasures of the kingdom and the way to the great adventure is found in study and researching things like church history?" a young man asked.

"I think that is one kind of treasure and one kind of adventure. For some, the greatest treasure is to see the works of the Lord done through them, leading others to salvation, healing, and doing miracles. For others, it is seeing God's people built together into His temple, the *koinonia* fellowship of the saints. For still others, it is prophetic experiences and being given prophetic insights into the future.

"The thread that runs through all great adventures is seeing the glory of the Lord in what He does through men and through us personally. These are all available to all of us, but for me personally, I found great treasures of knowledge in my studies of history, especially church history, and it was a great adventure to follow Him down that path. I saw and learned His ways as He personally taught me. It was one of the most fulfilling and thrilling times of my life until now, because I was getting to know Him this way."

"You said, 'Until now.' What are you doing now that is better?" one asked.

"As wonderful as it has been to see the Lord's ways as they are revealed in Scripture and history, to see Him working with actual people, with each of you here and now, is even better. I know we're just starting out, and we don't know each other very well yet, but already I can see . what great treasures you are. I think that if we have time to really get to know each other we will find a great treasure in every person. Then, we will begin to see how each one is being fit together into the city of God."

"We enjoyed our fellowship when on the ship and felt a bonding together, but never really had the concept that we were being built into something together, like the temple of the Lord or His city. Now I can see it," one remarked.

"For all of its failings and present shortcomings, there is no entity on the planet as dynamic and interesting as the church that is becoming what it is called to be. There is no greater society than true church life—*koinonia*; there is hardly anything as boring as church life that has been institutionalized, that has stopped pursuing the great sojourn that the true Christian life is. You are blessed to have been in the company of those who are committed to the journey."

"I consider myself very blessed," another replied. "The fellowship we had on the ship had become the best part of my life, but now being on this journey together is far better, even though it has been pretty frightening at times. If the mountain is even better than this, I just cannot imagine it."

"The Scripture says that the path of the righteous gets brighter and brighter until the full day. If we stay on the path we are called to walk our lives will keep getting brighter and brighter. We'll have challenges and trials like we've already had on this journey, but each one is filled with light, with revelation. Each one usually results in a much greater bonding among those with whom you experience them. I think that is why James wrote that we should *count it all joy when we encounter various trials.* If we approach each trial as the opportunity that it is, our journey will always lead to glory and victory."

"You're an old hand at this, aren't you?" another asked. "What are the most important things you've learned that can help us?"

"I've been through many wildernesses, and I've been through this part of this one before, so I do have some experience on these journeys," I replied. "It is a principle that between the place where you receive a promise from God and the fulfillment of the promise, there is always a wilderness to go through to get to the fulfillment. Each wilderness is unique, and each one designed to prepare us to be a good steward of what we've been promised. The real work of God to fashion us into what we are called to be is done in the wilderness. If we appreciate the trials and embrace the lessons He's seeking to teach us, we will get out of the wilderness quicker to receive what has been promised."

"What is the greatest thing you have ever learned in a wilderness?" another asked.

"Learning that we can all be as close to God as we want to be. It was in the wilderness that God's first dwelling place among men was built. It is in the wilderness that we are made into His dwelling place. Where He is, is heaven, so building Him a place to dwell with us can turn any wilderness into part of heaven. The worst place on earth will be heaven if He is there. This is our ultimate purpose—to bring heaven to earth—and we do this by building Him a place everywhere we go."

"Is that why Israel would carry the Ark of God with them into battle?" one asked.

"I think it was their intent. When they followed the Ark, going where the Lord was leading them, they always found victory. But, when they tried to take the Ark where they wanted to go, the results were not very good. We must learn that the temple exists for the Lord, not the other way around. We are here to follow Him, not just take Him with us. We are told that Christ will always lead us in His triumph, but that is the key—to let Him lead us rather than us trying to lead Him to where we want to go."

"What is the best thing we can do to help each other?" another asked.

"Just as we must be intentional about getting closer to the Lord and accomplishing our purpose in Him, we must be intentional about getting to know one another and seeing our purpose with one another. None of us is here by accident. We are called to be built together into the temple of the Lord; this is what we were made for, and we can never be truly fulfilled until this is complete. The process can be hard, but it can also be one of the most interesting and exciting things in our life.

"The first thing that God said was not good about His creation was for man to be alone. Loneliness is not good for any human being. We should consider that God said this when man had daily fellowship with Him. Fellowship with God is essential for man, and our most basic need, but God also obviously made man to need more than just fellowship with Him. His first provision for loneliness was family. After that, the greatest provision is our relationship to one another as members of His body.

"Going through this wilderness together will accomplish many things in us. The best of all will be how we get to know Him better. The next will be how we get to know one another better, so that we fit together as He has called us to be in His temple, as living stones. This is even more interesting and fulfilling than the great adventure I had as a student of history."

"So, until now, studying and research was your main thing, and now you're going to study us?" Mary, who had joined the group, asked. "I'm good with that. It does sound wonderful to get to know the Lord as your Teacher, but if you are going to answer my questions, I guess I will not be able to experience that in the same way."

"Sure you can. You all can, and should. Most of you already do. The time is now short, and you may not have the years to do this that I did, but you can experience the same thing with Him. It could be even better for you because it can be more condensed, but this is something you must all do. He must be your Teacher, Shepherd, and Leader.

"I think it is one of the Lord's chief delights to share with His people the treasures of wisdom and knowledge. Curiosity is a wonderful gift to have, and this is why I think answering your questions is so important for our journey. He may teach you faster because you do not have the time that I did, but it can be no less special and personal. If I have the answers to some of your questions it is because He put me here for you. Others here may have your answers, and they were put here for you as well."

As the sun began to set, we found a place near the stream to camp. We posted watchmen and then drank our fill until all were refreshed. We then built a fire that everyone gathered around. Some began talking in small groups. William came over to sit by me.

"I was listening to your conversation with that group. Their hunger for knowledge is contagious. Is everyone on this journey so exceptional?" William asked.

"It seems that they are. It takes uncommon faith and vision to begin this journey. Even those who might have lived rather mundane and unremarkable lives come alive and become exceptional here.

"Every day is different on this path. You can't fall into a routine and become an automaton here. You have to be alive and engaged. We were created for adventure. Life is meant to be an adventure, and this is the greatest of all adventures."

"Every day so far has been unique and fascinating," William continued. "Every person is unique and fascinating. I have not felt this exhilarated since I was a new graduate just starting out in my professional life. In fact, this is much better than that."

"Everything that you have done before in your life was preparation for this," I added. "This is where everything that has happened in our lives starts to make sense. The mountain is where it all comes together."

"If all of this, and everything that has happened in our lives, is but preparation for the mountain, it has to be the most extraordinary experience we could ever have," William said.

"I assure you, there is nothing else in this life that can compare to what you will experience on the mountain. The Lord did not say that we would be given a life of abundance, but rather an abundant life. Having an abundance of life does not mean that it is all good or easy, but that there is a lot of it.

"Here life becomes focused, condensed, and everything crammed with meaning. The mountain makes everything we have been through in life and on this path not only worth it, but useful. This is where we are being fashioned into what we are called to be, but the mountain is where we will function in what we are called to be."

"This is so different from anything I've experienced or heard of since becoming a Christian. I feel that this is real Christianity, that this is the way it should be for those who are serving the King of kings. Is this the true faith?" William asked.

"I think it is where faith becomes true. It no doubt takes faith to stay in a lukewarm or dead institution and remain faithful to the Lord. Those who do may be growing as much in the Lord as we are here. Others who are in jobs or places where it is a battle every day to remain faithful could be growing as we are here.

"These can be in their wilderness experiences and be on paths that lead to the mountain as long as they are on the sojourn to find the city of God. But if they are remaining where they are in order to take the path of least resistance or least risk, doing this more out of a lack of faith, I think they have been led astray."

"You mentioned that there will be paths along our way that will offer different, easier ways that will actually be a distraction or deception," William interjected.

"There will be many traps and distractions," I replied.

"The distractions or paths that lead us astray are almost always a temptation to take the easier way, aren't they?"

"Yes. If we choose any path out of a concern for ourselves, we will likely be led astray. We must make every decision based on the purposes of the kingdom, seeking the kingdom first, or we will depart from the right path. That is principle number one when we have a choice of paths.

"Another important principle is that we must not look back. Until we make the decision that we will not go back, regardless of how painful it gets, we will not go forward with the force of faith that it will take to choose the right way. If we are still looking back, we are not ready to go forward. The one with true faith views even the most severe obstacles as opportunities to win greater victories and make a greater advance toward his goal. True faith makes a road where there is none."

"So principle number one is '*seek first the kingdom*' with every choice. The second is '*forgetting what lies behind, press on toward the mark of the high calling of God.*'" These two will help us make the right choices," William recounted.

"These are the two basics that must guide our choices. Now, if anything happens to me, you can help these get to the mountain."

"You say this as if you're expecting something to happen to you. I am a novice in the Lord. You don't expect me to take your place if something did happen to you?" William replied.

"I'm not expecting anything to happen to me, but we need to be prepared. As Mark said when he first joined us, you are a leader, and if you needed to, you could get these through this wilderness," I answered.

"The attack of the lion shook you up, didn't it?" William countered.

"It did make me think of what would happen to these if something happened to me. I think you could make it through very well if it did. I just want you to be ready if something happens to me."

"I would do whatever I could to help these people, but I am far from ready to be a leader here," William protested.

"William, you will never be ready. I am not ready for this. I am in way over my head. If we are on the right path we will always be beyond our own wisdom and abilities. That keeps us seeking the Lord, depending on Him, and staying close to Him. You will never feel adequate if you are in the place He has set you, because you will never be adequate within yourself."

William had exceptional spiritual wisdom and discernment for being such a new believer. He had left behind a life of remarkable position and privilege to enter this wilderness just as the first sojourner, Abraham. I pondered how I had recently almost fallen to the same trap that Elijah did in thinking I was alone. Obviously, the Lord had some of His best men and women making ultimate sacrifices to pursue Him and to join Him in what He was building. There may not be many yet, but they were exceptional.

As I was pondering this, another group approached with some questions.

"You've been in this wilderness for a while," a lady in her late thirties or early forties began. "This is like living in another world. It's like we've begun to live in the most wonderful adventure novel or movie, or even better. It is like we are being prepared to live another Book of Acts. Is this normal Christianity? Is this the way life is supposed to be?"

"What is your name?" I asked.

"Jennifer, but most call me Jen."

"I will answer your question with a question," I began. "Do you think that what we see on the news is a reflection of real life?"

"No. Only the most extreme or exceptional events or people make the news. What makes the news is but a small part of what is happening in a day," she answered, looking at me as if she wanted to know what this had to do with our conversation or her question.

"That is right," I began. "The news can be helpful in keeping us informed about major issues and events, but it is not the reality most people are experiencing. Likewise, the events and people that make it into Christian publications and Christian television are like the news in many ways. They may be the exceptional, but they are just a tiny fraction of all that is going on in Christianity.

"Christian publications and programs focus on great churches, great missionaries, great missions, great artists and musicians, but altogether I think these are less than one percent of the true work of the kingdom. The majority of churches do not stand out like that, yet they are doing the majority of the work of the kingdom by being faithful in their daily walk with God—witnessing, teaching, praying, counseling, and seeking to build others up and help them find their way to the kingdom.

"For several years, I asked every large gathering of Christians that I could how many had come to the Lord through a crusade, Christian television, or evangelistic campaigns. Less than two percent of those I asked had come to the Lord through these means. All of the rest, over ninety-eight percent, had come to the Lord through the witness of a friend or relative. So where is the real work of the kingdom going on? Is it with the great ministries and campaigns, or with faithful believers who are daily being faithful?"

"It is with faithful believers who are daily being faithful to witness," Jen replied. "I still don't make the connection between this and my question. Is this real Christianity the way it is intended to be?"

"What you are experiencing here is real, biblical Christianity. What others are experiencing, that may be at a much slower pace and far less spectacular, can also be real Christianity. The time that you spent in what now seems like unreal and unsubstantial Christian life did help prepare you for the path you are now on.

"I have traveled the world and the church world about as much as anyone I know, but I am continually encountering huge movements and streams in the body of Christ I never knew existed. The body of Christ is big, and even those who may have traveled as extensively as I only see part of it. I have begun to see every expression of Christianity as a possible on-ramp for those who would seek this path to the city of God.

"If we are going to perceive truth and walk in it, we must keep in mind we only see in part and know in part. Do you remember when they put the Hubble telescope in orbit? This allowed astronomers to see further into the heavens than had ever been seen before. They focused the telescope on some stars and saw that what they thought was a star was actually a galaxy with billions of stars. Instantly, the universe was many times bigger than we ever thought. The universe was always that big, but we didn't have the eyes to see it until the Hubble. When you get to the mountain you will have a similar experience seeing just how big and how diverse the body of Christ is."

"That's interesting," Jen retorted, "but I'm still having trouble making the connection."

"Being on this path is also like that. It is hard, and it is dangerous, and it is a place of revelation where your vision and your heart are constantly enlarged with such intensity that it's easy to see anything less as not being real. We've just started on the path, and it is easy to think that everything we did before was shallow and insignificant in comparison, but it is all a part.

"This is not to imply that some, and maybe most, at this time are trapped in a form of Christianity that is not real. Just as biology teaches that anything that stops growing starts dying, if we are on the path of life, we will constantly be expanding and growing.

"I think the first person to look through the Hubble must have been astonished at how limited his vision had been before. Walking here is like looking every day through a more powerful lens. Here you begin to see everything from a different perspective. Then, when you get to the mountain it is magnified many times over. All of this has been here, and we could have walked this path at anytime, but we did not see it until now."

"That is how I have felt every day we have been on this path. It is challenging and humbling, but wonderful. Why are there so many more people on the ship than here?" William asked.

"It is as the Lord said, this path is narrow, and few are finding it. When you look at the glamour and opulence of the luxury ship and then at this path, it is a wonder any would choose this path. You would never choose it unless your spiritual eyes have begun to open. In a sense, we have to be taken out of the mundane life of earth and taken to a spiritual orbit, like the Hubble, before we can see. As we walk this path it is not what we see in this wilderness, but what is taking place inside of us that is being magnified. Our hearts are being enlarged, because we are seeing more each day with the eyes of our heart."

"So why could we all of a sudden see and the others on the ship couldn't?" another asked.

"You had begun to set your heart on things above instead of the things on this earth. This is what begins to open the eyes of your heart, your spiritual eyes."

"Is that what it means that '*Many are called, but few are chosen?*'" William interjected.

"Yes. Everyone is called, but not many respond to the call. Not many go on to make their calling and election sure."

"I have experienced even more opulence than was on that ship, and I would not trade any of my experiences in the world for what I have already received on this path," William added. "I'm alive again. In fact, I am so alive now I wonder if I was ever truly alive before. I merely existed before. Now these people with us have become like the stars they focused the Hubble on. I'm sorry, but before I would hardly have paid attention to any of them, and now I see more in them than I've ever seen in people before. It's like what was seen through the Hubble—each one was a star that I now see is a whole galaxy."

"The eyes of your heart are opening, William. Even the least of these could lead millions to the kingdom. Others here may not lead people, but rather give vision to an entire field of knowledge, such as a science, opening the eyes of all who see through such things as biology or physics, to the One who created it all. There will be some who are now on this path, or soon will be, who will give single messages with such power that nations are transformed.

"This has happened at different times in history, but on a small scale. Those were all seeds, and now we're coming to the harvest. There was an evangelist in the early American colonies called 'Johnny Appleseed.' He used to say you can count the seeds in an apple, but you can't count the apples in a seed. Faith is like that seed.

"Here's the point. Reality is the universe was always as big as we're now coming to see it, but we could not see it. Our reality was, at one time, so small that we thought the sun and stars all revolved around the earth. Now we know differently. Just as our eyes are being opened to the true extent of the natural world, we are also being opened to the extent of the spiritual realm. It's always been there, but few have seen it, and few have lived in this reality."

"Why aren't churches leading their people here? Churches need transforming messages preached to them as well. It is true that I have not seen many, but I have visited quite a few. In none of them did I find such a reality as I have found here. How can they continue to grow so large while being so shallow?" another asked.

"I have read and listened to some of the great preachers of just a few decades ago. Today, you don't hear the kind of transcendent messages that they preached. In general, we seem to be getting more and more shallow," another commented.

"That may be true, but back up just a few months before you began gathering as the Society of Bonhoeffer. When you first began to gather, you were taking your first steps toward the mountain and did not even know it. All over the body of Christ right now there are many on-ramps that people are beginning to find that will lead them here, just as you were led here. You may be ahead of them in time, but that is so you can become servants who can help them.

"Even though you may not have found them yet in your limited experience in the body of Christ, there are great churches that are gateways to the kingdom, preparing their people for this path. They will soon find it, and they will be a part of the last battle.

"But you are right, most of the church world has been built more with modern advertising techniques than with the substance and power of the kingdom. Almost all people now, including Christians, have been conditioned to respond more to hype than truth. You can build the biggest churches and the biggest ministries with good marketing, but is the Lord in them? Can you find Him there?

"The Lord will bless many things He will not inhabit. He will even visit places He will not inhabit. But where is that place, the people, in whom He will dwell?"

"It's interesting that you would put it like that," William replied. "This has confused me a great deal in the services we had on the ship. I rarely felt drawn to God and rarely felt God in those meetings. I did, at times, but it was rare.

"I kept attending, hoping I would feel Him again, but most of the time I only felt people just getting excited about principles. Even when the messages were great, I rarely felt drawn to God in those meetings. I felt more compelled to learn principles. I know principles can be important, but this did not really satisfy my soul.

"I had already considered leaving the ship when I met that little group in the Society of Bonhoeffer. Even though I had nowhere else to go I could not bear to waste any more of my time there, until I met these seekers. I soon learned that the fire in them was really fueled by knowing about this path and determining to find it and walk it. Now we're here. They did what they said they would do, and it is already much better than I ever expected."

"What is in your heart, what you are seeking, is what man was created for—fellowship with God Himself. We are created to be His dwelling place. We will never be at peace or fulfilled until we dwell in Him and He in us.

"Christ was born in a stable. He is still being born in stables—some of the most humble, unlikely places. Just as it was with His birth in Bethlehem, you still need revelation to find Him. I assure you that there are many small, hidden, and usually very humble places where you can find Him, where He is dwelling. That is where most of the messengers of power who will lead His people to Him are being prepared.

"Understanding this is crucial, but we must also keep in mind that the Lord also dwelt in one of the most audacious temples ever built, where everything was overlaid with pure gold. He is big enough and diverse enough to be in both. Can we have big enough vision to see Him in both?"

"You're trying to get us to see Him in all places," William commented.

"That's exactly what we must do. We can't just see people or institutions where they are, but where they are called to be. Then we must help get them there. To see the Lord, we must sometimes have the vision that Simeon and Anna did, able to see in a mere infant the salvation of the world. We often miss Him because we are looking for Him as we expect Him to be, rather than as He is.

"This is why the two men on the road to Emmaus could not recognize Him when He drew near to them. It says, '*He appeared to them in a different form.*' I think the main reason we often miss Him when He tries to draw close to us is that we expect Him in a familiar form, and

He comes in a different form to help deliver us from our prejudices and opinions.

"I'm sorry if I reacted a little strongly Jen, but we can't start seeing the path we are on now as the only 'real Christianity.' The men on the road to Emmaus would have recognized Jesus if they had known Him after the Spirit instead of just after appearances. One of the main things we must learn in this wilderness is to see further, deeper, and wider than we have seen before, or we will continue to miss the Lord and the great opportunities He's given to this generation."

"No, this is helpful," Jen replied. "No doubt I was starting to go down a wrong path with my thinking. This path is such a drastic contrast to my whole previous experience that I was already becoming proud."

"Jen, you are, according to Proverbs, a wise person. Stay that correctible, and you will stay on the path. We cannot start thinking of ourselves as better than any others, or we will fall. If we have been given more grace, it is still more grace. He gives His grace to the humble and resists the proud. We can quickly go from God's grace to God's resistance, if we go that way."

It was a long time before anyone said anything else. I did not want to talk too much and wondered if I already had. It was so refreshing to be with so many interesting and spiritually hungry people. William finally spoke and confirmed to me that I was trying to say too much:

"Today may not have been as exciting as some days, such as when we had the lion attack, but it's been like trying to drink out of a fire hydrant. I've been trying to take notes on what I've been learning, and I can't write fast enough," he complained, but with a smile.

"I apologize for trying to get in too much, but I blame all of you for it," I responded. "You are too interesting and too interested."

"We would like to hear more," Mary spoke up.

"I would like to add one more thought about what we've been discussing," I continued. "The church drifted from its course for most of the church age. This began when God's people started worshiping the temple of the Lord more than the Lord of the temple. Some started worshiping individual truths more than the Truth Himself. All of this led to a great shipwreck from which we are still recovering. Regardless of what kind of church we are a part of, we will suffer shipwreck if we start esteeming our group, our church, as more important than others who are different from us.

"Jen, remember our little discussion about how most news stories are not normal life, but rather the exception? You are now living in the exception. You are making the news every day in heaven. This is the path to the high calling of God in Christ. Even so, we cannot think of ourselves as better or more important than others, but as servants of those who may not have had our experience. If we don't do this, we too will stumble and drift from our course. We are being prepared to go back and get many others and bring them to this path. We will not be able to do this if they sense arrogance in us.

"The best way we can help those who are trapped in something less than what we are now experiencing is to get to the mountain and help build the highway that the rest can travel on. When you go back to them you will go back with authority. You will represent a higher reality, another realm. Many will see it and will come.

"You are just the beginning of a great harvest, the greatest there has ever been. However, the fastest way for us to depart from the highway that is being built to prepare the way for the Lord is to become proud of the grace we have been given."

## CHAPTER ELEVEN

# THE REASON

"You often use the term 'true church.' Does this imply that there is a false church?" William asked.

"There is a true and a false church, both of which are prophesied in the Scriptures, and both of which we have all around us," I answered. "There is true and false with almost everything: true and false apostles, true and false prophets. We are even warned about 'false brethren.' The wheat and tares are mixed together now and will not be separated until the end. Learning to distinguish between the wheat and the tares is part of our curriculum. Learning to discern between the true and the false church is part of our curriculum."

"How do we distinguish the true church from the false?" William asked.

"You could answer your own question. You have already chosen, and you followed the true. There are not many who can make this distinction now, or there would be more who are on this path," I replied.

"It seemed that yesterday you were implying that all churches and institutions could be on-ramps to this path and to the mountain of the Lord. I am a bit confused," William said.

"This is true. The false church now has many of the true sojourners in it. Right now they are like David serving the house of Saul. They will be persecuted and driven out, but this experience will be one of the primary events of their life to help prepare them for what they are called to do.

"At the present time, the false church is more mature in being what makes it false than the true church is in what it is called to be. The leadership of what is about to come is still immature like David was when he began to serve in the house of Saul. Because the true is still immature it is hard to distinguish it now, but you will find it in places like you did with this Society of Bonheoffer. Even so, the wheat and tares look alike until both have matured. Only then will the difference really be seen.

"Let me share with you a couple of other distinctions between the true and false. The main purpose of the true church is to be the temple of the Lord, so the main thing that we should look for in the church is the presence of the Lord. When the Lord is in His temple it does not matter what the temple looks like. If the Lord is in it even the most glorious temple will not be what attracts your attention. If the temple is receiving all of the attention then it can only be because the Lord is not in it. The way we find the true church is not by looking for the church, but by looking for the Lord.

"The Lord will bless many things He will not inhabit. The mature have learned to look beyond just what He may be blessing to what He is inhabiting. It is one thing to be in a congregation where there is good teaching, worship, and ministry, but it is something else when you feel the Lord moving among people, and where He is the true focus of attention.

"Many worship the things of God instead of the God of all things. Some worship His truths more than Him. Some even worship, worship. This is sometimes just immaturity, but there is a difference when the teaching, preaching, worship, and ministry all come out of His presence.

"Likewise, if my ministry is getting more attention than the Lord is, I should be concerned that I have departed from my main purpose. I have learned the vanity of just trying to build a ministry or influence, even when it is for good reasons. When we mature we will want to help prepare the way for the Lord by helping to prepare His people for Him. If I am only increasing people's attention on me I am failing in my most important mission."

"I can see what you're saying," William responded. "Elijah is an example of what you're talking about. If I had imagined what he would look like I'm sure I would have thought he would be more impressive than he is. You can tell that he is never trying to draw attention to himself, but he would rather hide than be seen. When he appears it is only to help us along this path. You identify with that, don't you?" William asked.

"I guess I do," I replied. "I do not feel comfortable being the focus of attention. I would much rather lead in a hidden way, by helping to steer people toward their destiny rather than being out in front, even with a small group like this."

"Why is that?" William probed.

"I don't really know. This kind of leadership is a burden to me. I am doing this out of obedience, but it's not comfortable."

"If you don't mind, I'd like to talk more about your leadership. I know the leadership in the kingdom is supposed to be different, but you are more different than I was expecting. Do you mind if I ask you some personal questions, just for my own instruction?"

"No. I'm glad to answer them, if they will be helpful for you, but I would not hold myself up as a great example of kingdom leadership."

"Is your discomfort with leadership because you don't feel adequate for the leadership you have been called to?" William asked.

"I like your direct style. My answer to your question is that feeling inadequate could be a reason why I don't feel comfortable in this role, but I don't think that is it. I was told that feeling inadequate is a good thing and that if I ever started feeling adequate then I would be dangerous, so I've accepted that," I replied.

"At first, I interpreted your lack of comfort in your position as you not wanting to be with us or that you were just burdened by us," William commented. "I think that some of the group may feel that way, except those you spent so much time talking with yesterday. That was very helpful for them, not just by what you said, but your being so willing to talk with them."

"I'm sorry that any would feel that I don't want to be with them. That is really the opposite of what I feel. The more I have gotten to know everyone in this group, the more interesting you have all become. I am thoroughly enjoying you and the rest of them. Trust me, it is far more enjoyable going through this wilderness with you than it was going alone.

"I know, at times, I can be a clumsy person socially. I take a bit of comfort in the fact that Elijah seems to be even more so, but that too could be the secret of his power. He has learned to lean on the Lord, putting all of his trust in Him. I want to do the same. Being in leadership makes me lean on Him more than anything else I know. So I do embrace it even if I don't feel comfortable with it.

"I have learned to embrace feeling inadequate because I know it is actually the result of being inadequate. No person is capable of doing what they are called to do without God's help. That is why we were given the Helper. Feeling constantly inadequate makes you learn to lean on and trust in the Lord, to constantly seek Him. I embrace this as an opportunity, but I still don't enjoy being in leadership."

"So you never wanted to be a leader?"

"I think I did want to be a leader when I was young. I remember imagining what it would be like, and what I would be like as a leader. When it became a reality I was not nearly as good in reality as I was in my imagination. As a leader your successes are multiplied, but so are your failures. I have had some obvious successes, but I have also had some glaring failures in leadership. Some failures can make you lose faith, but that only proves it was a false faith in ourselves instead of faith in God."

"So to you, leadership is a burden?"

"Yes, but don't misunderstand me, I know it is the greatest honor and privilege we can have to be a leader of God's people. I am very thankful for this opportunity, but at the same time, I don't think I am very good at it.

"I have been a captain of thousands, and now it seems like I have been demoted back to being a captain of tens, given the job of leading a few dozen of you through this part of the wilderness. I'm good with that. I think these few dozen people on this path could have a bigger impact than the thousands I was leading before, so I know I have really been given a promotion.

"But as for leadership, I have been in some form of leadership almost my entire adult life, and I have never been more uncomfortable with it than I am now. It is a cross for me and I do, at times, long for a situation where I can just follow someone else. Right now that is not my part, so I want to be as faithful as I can with this."

"You said that you feel clumsy at times in personal relationships. That's the root of shyness, but I don't think your discomfort is the typical lack of self-confidence," William observed. "I think some of it is having been a captain of thousands and now being with a small group again. I've observed that those who are comfortable speaking to large audiences are often shy in small groups. Those who may be uncomfortable speaking to large groups can be comfortable in small groups. It's a different gift."

"I know that's true. I am very comfortable speaking to large groups, and feel awkward with small groups, but I enjoy the small groups much more even if I feel more uncomfortable with them."

"I've also observed you with Elijah. When we learned who he was, we were all quite intimidated, except for maybe Mary. Even Mark was a bit intimidating to us when we saw his gift. But you seemed to feel quite comfortable even with Elijah," William continued. "As much as I have been around powerful people I must admit that I still have a fear of them."

"I've known many of the successful and powerful in many fields so I'm used to being around high-impact people, but I think something else helped me even more not to fear people. I have seen the King, and it's hard to be impressed by anyone when you have seen Him," I responded.

"I think you are humble. I think you're humble in a good way that keeps you seeking the Lord and dependent on Him," William continued.

"I hope you're right. How can anyone see the King and not be humbled? I have wondered if my lack of fear of others was just arrogance, and I do see a lot of arrogance in my life so I don't want to rule that out. But I sincerely desire to have the kind of humility that God will give His grace to. I know I need His grace, and I think it was His grace that has allowed me to see Him as much as I have.

"It is a great advantage to have seen the glory of the Lord. How could I ever think too highly of myself or want to have people's attention on me after I've seen Him? In the presence of the Lamb even the twenty-four elders cast their crowns at His feet. Who could presume to be worthy of glory or attention in His presence? Who could presume leadership in the presence of the King of kings? In His presence there will not be presumption.

"I've also seen the great ones on the mountain. I've studied the great ones in history and in Scripture. We have a long way to go yet to measure up to those who have gone before us, but soon some of the greatest of all will emerge in the full maturity of all those who have gone before them. Some of these in this little band might be the ones."

"Were you told this or is this from biblical prophecy?" William inquired.

"Both. The Lord has saved His best wine for last, for the end of this age. Even if we get to walk in the fullness of what is coming, to presume glory or position after seeing Him would be more profane than anything I could think of. As I said, I've met many of the world's great leaders and successful people, and I try to give honor to whom honor is due, but it is hard to be impressed with anyone after you have seen the King. It is even more difficult to be impressed with yourself.

"I also want to be candid about my own flaws and mistakes to those I'm leading. We must build everything in this fellowship on truth. What I share about myself is true. It may be a lack of self-esteem or self-worth that makes me cringe when people give me too much attention, but it is also feeling that they are not seeing the Lord if they are looking too much at me. I understand that this may be natural for a time, but if it continues I am failing at the main thing I am called to do—to lead people to the King.

"One leader of a large movement once told me that I would never be a successful leader because I did not have 'warm fuzzies' that would attract people to me. That may be true, but I do not want to attract people to me. That is actually an appalling thought to me. My goal is to be successful at the job I've been given, and that job is to prepare them for the King's service and to follow Him. My personal goal is to hear on that great Judgment Day, '*Well done good and faithful servant.*'

"I know that may sound severe, but when I saw the King, I knew there was no higher calling than this—to prepare the way for the Lord and to lead His people to Him. There is no greater joy or fulfillment than this. I may at times chaff under the pressure that comes with always being in a place beyond my ability, but I know very well that this is the greatest job anyone could ever have. Since He put me here, I know He will supply what I need. I've also learned that my identity and value is not in my position before men, but my position in Him."

"So you are never threatened by those who want your position?"

"I assure you that I would probably give it away too easily if it were mine to give. Because this has been assigned to me I can only give it up when instructed by the One who gave it to me. If I do my job well then this will come sooner rather than later, so I will rejoice when it comes."

"I'm sorry to keep pressing you about this, but this is a kind of leadership that is so foreign to my whole experience that I cannot stop thinking about it. I see the wisdom, peace, and rest that would come from this. I see how this type of kingdom authority centered in the King could be the only way that true power could be given to men that would not corrupt them," William stated.

"This path will humble us all. If you stay on this path your veils, facades, pretenses, and selfish ambition will be removed. Then we can see His glory. When we see His glory with an unveiled face, we will be changed into His same image. If we see Him with the veils still on He will be distorted, and we will try to change Him into our image. This path is to get us ready to behold His glory by removing the veils."

I felt a presence and turned to see both Marys, Mark, and a number of others standing nearby listening.

"Please come join us," I said.

"Tell us more about seeing His glory," the older Mary said.

"I am happy to do this," I started. "These are my greatest memories, and I love to recount them. I have seen the Lord twice in person. I have seen Him numerous other times in dreams and visions, but seeing Him in person is different."

"How is it different?" The older Mary asked.

"It would be like the difference between watching someone in a movie and seeing them in person. You are seeing them act in the movie, but you are not really in their very presence.

"Even though I have seen the Lord twice with my physical eyes, you don't have to see Him with your physical eyes if your spiritual eyes have been opened. Even when He does not become visible to our natural eyes being in His manifest presence is the greatest experience we can have. Nothing else on earth can ever satisfy you like being in the manifest presence of the Lord. Because we were created to have fellowship with God this is the deepest yearning of the human heart, and nothing else can ever compare to it."

"I think I've had tastes of that, but not like you are describing," the older Mary continued. "I would like to. Sometimes I think that if I could just see the Lord or an angel, then I would not have so many questions."

"Mary, that may be true, but I think He wants you to have those questions. I think you are called to know the deep things of God, and He has put in you a searching heart that will not accept superficial answers.

"I don't think the things I've experienced happened because I am special. I think just about anything I've experienced can be received by anyone who wants them enough to seek Him for them. I started asking for these experiences when I was a new Christian. When I read about them in Scripture, I yearned for them so much I could not help but beg God for them. I did this for years before they started to happen, but it was worth the wait. It does not have to be years for you, but you have to want this enough to seek, to knock on His door, to pursue Him without giving up."

"Are you sure this does not happen to you because you have a special calling?" the younger Mary interjected.

"Some of it may be, but I also know this is something you can desire, and pursue, and receive. God wants the most intimate relationship with everyone, but He will only draw near to those who want Him enough to draw near to Him.

"As Mark can affirm, with prophetic experiences there are levels. There are visions that are so faint that you see them with the eyes of your heart so gently that you wonder if they are your imagination. Then there are those that are like watching a cinema screen.

"Likewise, I've felt Him come in a very subtle gentleness, seemingly just to comfort me or give me peace. Then I've felt His presence like a nuclear fire. It burned so much I do not think I could have lived much longer in it.

"When I experienced Him as the burning fire, it was not His anger but His holiness. We are told in Hebrews that He is a consuming fire. It hurts, but it hurts good. It was both painful and wonderful beyond description. I've had to beg Him to leave me at times because it was too much for me to take at the time. I was too carnal to stay in His presence long and not be consumed."

"Were the experiences you had seeing Him in dreams and visions like that?" Mark asked.

"Some were to a degree, but they were all different. Some dreams were gentle and subtle, and some were so real that I still remember them as if they had been an actual experience and not a dream.

"The experiences I had on the mountain, and in the mountain, were very impacting to me. The one on the top of the mountain was all glory, beauty, and a feeling of love and oneness like I had never experienced. When you get there it will make all of the battles and problems of this journey seem insignificant.

"The experience I had in the mountain when I witnessed His crucifixion was possibly even more impacting, but also one of the most painful and difficult experiences I've ever had. Even though I knew He was now risen and seated above all I grieved for days as if I had been there at His real crucifixion. I still marvel that the disciples who were there, and His mother, could have endured this. I know they were much stronger than I am."

"So we will all get to see His glory?" several asked at once.

"Yes. You will all see His glory, if we stay on this path. We are going to the mountain of the Lord. Even with all of the battles and conflicts there it is like no other place because His presence is there. Fighting for truth and the greatest cause is inspiring, but even these cannot compare to fighting for the One you love.

"The greatest reward we could ever receive is to be close to Him. That's why even the apostles disputed who would be the closest to Him. They did not want those positions just for the authority or the renown, but to be as close to Him as possible. It may have been selfish, but not self-centeredness. There is a difference.

"It is not wrong to seek to be great or to do great things for Him, which is why most begin this journey. But once you experience His manifest presence, once you see Him, everything changes. Then it becomes all about serving Him because He deserves it, not for what we get. Yet, we do receive more than we can even dream of. To bring Him joy for one moment is worth a lifetime of suffering many times over. When you see Him you will understand this."

"There is a weight to your words that could only come from you having been with Him," Mark offered.

"That's an interesting way to put it, Mark. The anointing has been described as the weight that comes from His glory. The Word says that all things are held together by Him. Weight is gravity, and gravity is what holds all things together. There is a weight to glory, and the more glory you experience the more weight your words will have.

"As you will see, just one moment in His presence will make all the battles of this wilderness worth it many times over. It will compel you to keep going through the many battles in the future. Even so, you are called to more than just battles. You will not only see His glory, but you are called to dwell in His presence and to manifest His glory in the earth. You are called to carry the glory of the Lord just as the priests carried the Ark of His Presence."

By this time, the rest of the group had all gathered and were listening. As I looked at them, I could not help but consider how unimpressive most of them were by just their natural appearance, yet they could all end up being some of the greatest souls to ever walk the earth.

"It is your calling to carry the glory of the Lord in the time of greatest darkness. Regardless of how dark it gets, we know that the glory will prevail. It is written, '*the nations will come to the brightness of your rising.*' I might share more later about my own experiences, but I am here to help get you ready for yours," I continued.

"Elizabeth Barrett Browning once wrote that 'Earth is crammed with heaven, and every common bush afire with God; but only he who sees takes off his shoes—the rest sit round it and pluck berries.' We are here to have our eyes opened and to see. You will see His glory and know His manifest presence, but His glory is all around us now, and He is with us now. We are not here to look for Him, but to look at Him. He is not in the creation as He is its Creator, but creation reveals Him, and we can see Him in everything when we learn to see.

"Jon Amos Comenius said that nature is God's second book. This may be true, but He has other books too. Seeing Him is more than seeing Him in creation; it is seeing Him in every experience. It is also seeing Him in one another. Everyone here is a letter from God to the rest of us. That is why our goal is not to just hear the words of the Lord, but to hear the Word Himself as He speaks to us through whomever or whatever He chooses.

"Jesus is the Word. He is the communication of God to His creation. If we were sensitive enough we would know that there is a communication between all living things. As we come to abide in Him we will start to know this communication. More important than hearing the creation is hearing the Creator speaking to us. He said in John 10 that His sheep hear His voice, and they follow Him because they hear His voice.

"Our purpose is to see Him, hear Him, and feel Him. Great lovers can feel the presence of their loved one when they come close, regardless of whether they can see or hear them. Love is spiritual gravity too. It is a force greater than gravity because God is love. Love between human beings can be magnificent, but there is no greater love than God's love, and loving God in return. This is why there is no person on earth more attractive or compelling than one who is getting closer to God.

"Jesus is the true desire of every human heart. When He is lifted up all men are drawn to Him. For too long we have tried to lift up the things of God rather than the God of all things. We have, at times, lifted up truths about Him, above Him. Those are coming who will lift Him up, and they will carry His glory so that He is seen. You could be the ones.

"The most common question that people have is about their purpose in life. The answer is that we are here to see Him, know Him, love Him, become like Him, and to reveal Him. If we do this we will fulfill the greatest purpose one can have on the earth. If we do this we will be the most successful human beings to ever walk the earth. Those who do this will be celebrated by the whole earth because they will have the power to help restore the earth to what it was created for. This is why it says '*the creation groans and travails waiting for the manifestation of the sons of God.*'

"He is the Truth. He is the most noble cause. We are not doing this just for ideals, but we are being prepared to serve the King who defines all truth, nobility, and all that is good. There is none more deserving of our devotion and our sacrifice. There is no greater cause than His, and there is no greater adventure than the path you are all on.

"And we have just begun."

## CHAPTER TWELVE

# THE TURNING

The terrain had become much more difficult. The living water was refreshing and energizing, but we had gone many days with no solid food. We looked for fruit trees, but had not found any. After we crested a particularly difficult hill, we were all weak. We could not even find the stream to drink from. As we sat resting, William came to sit next to me.

"I have thought a lot about our conversation on leadership, and as I told you, I'm glad to help in any way that I can," William offered.

"Is there something specific that you think you can do to help us?" I asked.

William continued, "I really care about these people, and I admit to being a little protective of them when you showed up, but I've come to trust you. However, there are some here that I do not trust."

"Please continue," I said. "I think you know these people much better than I do."

"There is a clique that has formed. It's mostly the young people and the youth. You have surely noticed how they stand off from the rest of the group now. I think they have their own agenda. I think that if we do not find water and food soon, they will break away and go off on their own. They could take many of the others with them."

"This is helpful to know," I said. "Have they caused any specific problems yet?"

"The only problem I think they've caused so far is to make some of the others uncomfortable. The problems people like that cause only come when other real problems surface." William said, looking at me with obvious and grave concern.

"How can we remedy this?" I asked.

"I'm so used to dealing with another generation, I don't know if I could be much help with them," William continued.

"They are important to us," I said. "We may be here more for them than they are here for us. Finding solutions and turning problems into solutions is essential for us to make it through this wilderness. If this is a major problem we have a major opportunity."

"Do you not think that some situations here are simply meant to be a trap?" Andrew, the young officer from the ship asked, who had come to sit with us.

"That is a good question, and I agree that there are situations here that are traps intended for evil. Even so, they have been allowed so that we can learn to overcome evil with good. Every one of them has something important to teach us. Andrew, were they this way on the ship too?" I asked.

"Yes they were, but as we started out on this journey they seemed to draw closer to the rest of the group. Then

I noticed them begin to drift apart again. One seems to have arisen as their leader, and I think he may be the cause of this."

"Let's go pay them a visit," I said.

The young adults and youth were just a little off to themselves and were about twenty-four in number. I had been observing them from a distance too, and one of them stood out as the obvious leader. As I looked at them now he was seemingly holding court with a semi-circle arrayed in front of him. Others were standing around behind him, but all were listening to what he was saying.

When I got near and greeted them, they all turned to me and gave me their attention, but it was not with a lot of enthusiasm. In fact, they reacted as if they thought I was going to scold them.

"We need your help," I began.

"How can we help you?" the leader asked.

"We need trained, skilled watchmen who have courage and discernment," I replied.

"We're neither trained nor skilled at being watchmen," one of them said.

"You may not be trained yet, but you are skilled. You have discernment and the kind of courage it will take to do this job," I said.

"What makes you think that?" the leader responded.

"I could not help but notice that when the lion attacked us most of you were not that afraid. You were not paralyzed like some of the others. In fact, you seemed ready to fight, even excited by the challenge of it. I started watching you then, and I could not help but see how perceptive you are.

"I also saw how interested you are in Mark and his gift. That's because many of you have the same gift. It will awaken in you on this journey if it has not already. You are drawn to the supernatural because you are called to a supernatural life, and you are being prepared for the last battle which will be supernatural. Many of you are called as prophets. The foundation of prophetic ministry is being a watchman," I said. "We are in need of watchmen, and you are in need of the experience."

Virtually the entire group had become much more interested, and some even enthusiastic. One of the girls seemed very unenthusiastic, so I asked her what she was thinking.

"My parents said that those who claim to be watchmen are almost all bitter, critical people who just sow division and discord in others," she said. "I was in a lot of rebellion to my parents, so I started listening to some of those who called themselves watchmen, and I even read some of their material. I have to admit that my parents were right. They seemed negative toward everyone and everything. I don't remember ever hearing any of them say anything good or positive about anyone. If we become like that, I do not think it will lead us to the mountain of the Lord," she said.

"That is an interesting and important insight," I responded, "That is just the kind of discernment we need. She is right about the critical spirit that is in many self-proclaimed watchmen. There are a number of reasons for this, but the main one could be that the people who have the gifts and callings have not taken their place, so others who are not called to do it fill the void.

"What is your name?" I asked the girl.

"Alexis," she replied.

"Alexis, you are obviously one who is committed to truth and depth if you were willing to search out what your parents said about this group. What else did you learn?"

"There is a bitterness and critical spirit in so many of them that it is a spiritual poison. It destroys and does not build up. I think it is rooted in unforgiveness, or having disappointments and wounds that never healed."

"Alexis, these are important insights," I continued. "There are unique traps set for every one of us here. To become overly critical and negative is a trap set especially for those who are called to be watchmen and prophets. Those who fall into that trap end up sowing fear and division instead of faith and love for God and one another. This poison can be much more deadly than all of the false teachers and false shepherds combined. What I am asking you to do is dangerous, but we need you.

"Not forgetting this warning that Alexis has brought to our attention, let me share some of the good things about this calling. We are called to walk by faith, not fear. We must be wise and discerning enough to see the traps, but our basic purpose is to look for the right path, not just the wrong ones. For this reason, the watchmen are usually the first to see the wonders and the glory.

"We are changed into the image of what we behold, and if we're just looking at and studying the enemy all of the time we can start to take on his nature. Biblical watchmen were also to be on the lookout for the coming of the King or His messengers, to warn the people of their approach so that they could have a proper reception prepared.

"It's true that critical people rarely build anything, but just tear down. Such may be stumbling blocks, but there would not be so many of those if the true called ones would rise up and take their place as watchmen for the body. We need those of you who are called to this to take your place and learn to do it the right way.

"It is not a small thing I'm asking of you. There is a lot of danger involved. You will be in the vanguard, and when there is danger you will be the first to face it. It will take a lot of courage, and it will take wisdom and discernment. Even though some of you are very young, you will have to mature quickly to do this job.

"What is your name?" I asked the apparent leader.

"My name is Charlie."

"Do you mind if I call you Charles?"

"No. I don't mind."

"Charles, would you mind acting as a leader of the watchmen?" I asked.

"I'm open, but why me?" he asked.

"Because you're a leader, and you're mature beyond your years. I also think you care enough for these people that you would not abandon them and would do what it takes to protect them," I replied.

"How do you know so much about me?" Charles asked.

"It is my job to know those who are with us," I replied.

After a long moment, Charles replied, "I'll help you get this going. I can see that having trained watchmen is going to be critical if we're going to make it through this place."

"All watchmen are critical, Charles, but your job will be even more so," I added. "You will have to watch out for the watchmen. You must be free to come to me any time to talk about anything that concerns you.

"I would also like to get to know all of you a little better. Do you mind if I ask you some questions?" I continued.

"No," several of them said.

"What were your reasons for coming on this journey and leaving behind such a comfortable ship?" I began.

Their reasons were varied, but a common thread was boredom. They needed adventure. Several wanted to get to know the Lord better. They said they were just hearing about Him on the ship, but they were not experiencing Him. The depth and sincerity of most of their answers was very encouraging, even to William and Andrew who were obviously impressed.

I then asked Charles to divide the group into teams of four each who would begin to stand watch with the men and women who had been volunteering as watchmen. I asked William to introduce them to those who were presently working as watchmen. As I got up to walk away, William and Andrew began a conversation with a few of them and remained behind.

After the meeting with the watchmen, we sent two groups to go before us down the hill to scout out the path and seek water. About an hour later messengers returned saying they had found an adequate place to camp for the evening, but still had not found water.

I was getting concerned that I had missed a turn and had led them on a wrong path. If this was the case we would have to go back to where we missed the turn. The wrong path will never become the right path, but will take you further and further from the right path. Going back is always discouraging, but it is at times necessary. The discouragement would be magnified if there was no food or living water to drink. I decided to discuss the situation with William, Andrew, and Charles.

Because none of us could think of any place where we could have diverted from the path, we resolved to keep going forward, at least to the place where we could camp for the night and maybe get a better perspective in the morning.

After settling at the campsite, William came over to sit by me.

"I never expected what you did with those kids today. Just giving them a part seems to have completely changed their attitude. They are not the kids I thought they were. I'm glad you saw more in them than I could see," he said.

"William, you were right about them. They were as you thought they were. They were in danger of separating themselves, and may have already done it if it had not been for the lion attacks. That attack got their attention, but they were only staying close to us out of fear. They may have had less fear than others, but they were alarmed by that attack. You did see the problem correctly, and I appreciate you bringing it up when you did."

"You are being gracious, but I remember what you said about having to see every problem as an opportunity. I know that as a basic leadership principle. I failed to see the opportunity in this. What they needed was to be shown respect, to be valued and given a purpose. I failed to see it," William lamented. "I would have begun by chewing them out for being so stand-offish and proud. I would have probably driven them away."

"Perhaps, but you won't the next time," I responded. "I did not go to them just to try to get them engaged with the rest of the group. We do need them. They are critical to all of us making it through this wilderness. To make it we need everyone in the right place doing what they were called to do.

"Those kids were excited by the lion attacks. Some of them panicked, which is to be expected, but most were ready to fight in spite of their fear. They loved the way Elijah went right after those lions. They're warriors. With some training and guidance they will be a powerful force by the time we get to the mountain.

"Now here is the part you still may not see—they need you, and you need them," I said.

"I would love to help them, but how? I stayed and talked with them for a while after you left. I felt like I was almost bonding with them. I was surprised by how I was drawn to them. I would never have expected it. So you think I am going to be able to help train them?" William asked.

"William, you too have gifts you do not know about yet," I replied. "They need a mentor, and you are not just a good one, you are the perfect one. There is leadership on all of those kids, and you are called to be a teacher to them. They will draw the living water out of you that you do not even yet realize is in you."

"I confess to being excited just to try," William replied. "What do I need to do next?"

"The foundation of all that we are called to be and do in God is family first. Relationship must be first. Get to know them. Let them get to know you. Relationships are built on trust and affection. However, they do not need you as another buddy, but as a father and, at times, a drill sergeant.

"You don't have to change to connect to them as you should, and they should not have to change to connect with you. Be yourself, and let them be who they are. We're all going to change on this journey, but it must be through the process of the experiences, not artificially. They will mature, and you will have some of your youth restored."

"That is very encouraging and liberating," William responded. "I am a bit repulsed when people my age try to act like teenagers. I am already so fond of these kids that I would have done it if I had to, but I think it would have been ugly."

"It would have been more ugly than we want to consider, but for us to fit together as we are called we all must be who God has made us into, and not try to be anything else. The trust and respect that all true relationships are built on begins with us trusting who we are and respecting ourselves enough to be real with one another. We are commanded to 'speak truth to one another,' which also means to be true, to be real with one another.

"One other thing about your relationship to these younger ones—I can see that just talking about this is awakening you. That's the living waters flowing in your heart. These living waters can only come out of our innermost being, our deepest heart desire. Our deepest heart desire touches what we were created for. When you touch that purpose, you open a well of living water in your heart.

We're following the living water here because it will lead us to the mountain. Follow the living water that flows from your heart the same way."

"You are right that I feel energized by just the thought of being able to connect with those kids. The thought of being a mentor to them is very exciting. But just this morning I did not even like them, and now it's like they're my favorite people. You knew this when you took me to talk to them, didn't you?" William asked.

"I suspected it," I replied. "I knew they needed you, and I assumed that you would also need them. I was hoping you would make a connection with them, but I cannot say that I was sure it would work out."

"Doesn't it always work out this smoothly when God has ordained something?" William said, more as a statement than a question.

"No. It does not always work out that smoothly or quickly even when it is His purpose. Sometimes, and I would even say most of the time, when things happen too easily or too fast they tend to be insignificant."

"Well, if we applied that to my relationship to these kids, then it would not be that important," William said, questioningly.

"William, there are laws, and there are principles. There are no exceptions to laws, but principles have exceptions. This is a principle that is, I think, true most of the time, but not always. Generally, the more you have to fight for something the more important or valuable it is, and the more important and valuable you will therefore consider it to be.

"However, I know you have a calling to be a mentor to the emerging generation. For this reason, even though the initial connection seemed to have been so fast and easy, I think you need to be very watchful of this relationship being tested, and maybe more severely than you would expect. Just don't be thrown off when the testing comes."

"I see your point. Sometimes the testing is not immediate, but it will come. To be forewarned like this can be very helpful. I will try to prepare for the testing so that I am not shaken when it comes," William replied.

I marveled at how teachable William was as I watched him walk off toward a few of the youth who were approaching, obviously wanting to talk with him. This connection was important, and maybe the most important thing that had happened to us yet. I also knew that getting the watchmen trained and in place was going to be more important every day.

I then turned my attention to the crisis at hand—food and water. The scouts had all come back with reports of finding nothing, and it was now too dark to send them out again. The more I sat thinking about it, the more all my fears about being a poor leader came cascading down upon me. This is the most basic need that people have, and I had led them to a place where their basic needs could not be met. I was getting distraught that I had already let them down.

As I looked around, most were falling asleep quickly because they were so exhausted. They would desperately need food and water in the morning. I was weak too, but I felt even worse about being the cause of it. For the first time since I had joined this group, I would have rather been going through the wilderness alone again. When I was alone my mistakes did not affect so many others.

I had not followed the most basic principle Elijah had told me—to never get far from the stream of living water. I wanted to sleep, especially knowing that the next day could be a very hard one, but sleep did not come. I would like to have discussed the situation with William, but he was still talking with a few of those we had assigned as watchmen. I started to think that there could not be a lonelier feeling than being a leader and feeling that you have led those in your charge badly.

I decided to get up and walk a little distance from the camp to pray. That is when I saw him, standing in the path directly in front of me.

## CHAPTER THIRTEEN

# THE SHEPHERD

I walked up to him and stopped a few feet away. He looked at me for a moment, took the staff that was in his hand, and tapped the ground.

"It's here," he said.

I looked down at the ground and could see a little trickle of water where he had struck it. I looked back at him, and he was smiling the most wonderful, friendly smile I think I've ever seen.

"I've come to show you this, and to give you this," he said, handing me the staff.

I looked at the staff. There did not seem to be anything unique or remarkable about it. It was just a straight stick about as long as I was tall. It seemed to have been freshly cut, and still had bark on it, so that I knew it had not been used much, if at all.

"It has not been used much," he began. "It was cut for you from the great tree. The cloak you wear for grace, but this you use for authority."

"I never thought I would have one of these," I replied. "Can I ask you a few questions about it?"

"Of course," he said with a smile that was so compelling and truly joyful that I felt almost completely at ease.

"You are very different from the way I thought you would be. I was not expecting you to bring me anything, but if I had, it would not have been this shepherd's staff. If there is anything I feel I have been a terrible failure at, it is being a shepherd. The fact that you have brought me this must be a message. Can you explain it?" I asked.

"The Lord's strength is made perfect in weakness. Your failures have prepared you for what you are now called to do.

"I was the first to walk with God after Adam. The more I sought Him the more He became my joy. Then the time I spent with Him became more desirable than anything in this world. Just being with Him was on my mind night and day. He became my life. This, too, is your desire.

"It is the foundation of a shepherd's life. You will only lead and care for His people well if you are walking with the Lord and getting ever closer Him. When you stop getting closer to Him you will begin to fail in your leadership of His people, because your purpose is to lead them to Him. He is their green pasture. He is their living water. He is their rest. He is their life," Enoch explained.

I could not help but stare at Enoch. I have never seen anyone so deeply joyful or full of love. I have never seen a smile that made you feel so good, so accepted, and valued. I just did not expect Enoch to be anything like this—perhaps the happiest person who ever lived! I then looked closely at the staff he had given me.

"I have been used to teach and prophesy, but I never thought I would ever be given this staff," I continued. "I know I have been called to lead people in different ways, as I am now leading this group through this wilderness, but I never saw myself as a shepherd. I'm honored but concerned. I intimidate people rather than make them feel comfortable.

"I don't want to be that way and don't like it, but I am and don't know how to change. Just being with you these few minutes, I would say that you are possibly the warmest person I've ever met. I am not making light of this. I consider that a great gift, one that is needed for this job and one that I do not have."

"What I have is the joy of the Lord," Enoch continued. "This is not a gift, but fruit. It is the fruit of walking with the One who is the greatest desire of every heart. The closer you walk with Him the more joy you will have. The joy that you have in Him then becomes a joy in His people, in His creation, and in everything He calls you to do.

"This is because you will be doing it with Him. Getting closer to Him will change you into who He made you to be. When you get closer to the consuming fire, then the warmth of His fire will be in you."

"These few days with this group has uncapped something deep inside of me," I replied. "Every day I care more for them. Something in me has changed so that I see them differently than I have seen a group of people before. Everyone is a priceless treasure. I just love being with them, and I'm more thankful for this job every day. I long for the mountain, but if the King was to keep me here leading groups through this part of the wilderness over and over, I would be happy," I admitted. "If this is why I am being given this staff, I am very happy about it."

"Every assignment given by the King is like that. It is while you are walking with Him and doing His work that the innermost springs of your heart are opened. Though you were called as one from the beginning, you did not come here as a shepherd, but you will leave here as one," Enoch said, taking me by the shoulders and smiling even more broadly. "Now, you have more questions. Please ask them."

"The water here is under our feet? Can I get it just as you did, by tapping the ground with this staff?" I inquired.

"Yes, you can. With this staff, you can tap the ground and waters will flow. You can even strike a rock, and waters will flow from it," he answered.

"So I do not have to stay close to a flowing stream anymore?" I asked.

"You must always stay close to the living waters, and they are always flowing, but here they are not on the surface. As you go into higher places like this you will often have to dig for the living water. The higher you go the deeper you may have to dig for them, but they will be near you. They will always be close to the path you are to walk," he added.

"So, if I stay on the right path we should always find the waters nearby?"

"Yes. In fact, they will be right under your feet. If you cannot find them under your feet then you know you have strayed from your course.

"The higher you go, the slower you must go, because you will have to dig deeper for water. This is by design.

This is a place of vision, and you must go slowly enough to see all that you are called to see.

"It is here in the high places that those who are with you must learn to see and to go deeper for the waters of life. If they cannot find the water, then you can help them with your staff, but do not help them too much. They are here to learn to go deep and to see."

"Is Elijah still with us?" I asked

"We are always together."

"Will they be able to see you and talk with you the way they have with Elijah?"

"They will. We will both be very close to you until you reach the mountain. We were the first, and the prototypes of the great messengers who are about to be released upon the earth. It is our honor to serve them and prepare them for the last battle.

"Then the whole earth will be restored to the paradise it was created to be, and all people here will know and serve the Lord. Then all mourning and pain will be over, and the joy of the Lord will be everyone's portion."

With that Enoch touched my head as if to bless me, nodded, and walked off. As I watched him go, I could not help but think he is the happiest man to have ever lived. I have met many joyful people, but none like him. He was the first to find the secret of true joy—walking with God. There are many who have had qualities I would like to have, but I have never wanted anything as badly as I did Enoch's joy. I had never felt so drawn to anyone before, so close or so comfortable in their presence. Just a fraction of his joy would make every day wonderful and would help me to make other people's days better.

Then I heard a familiar voice behind me.

"As he is, you can be also," Elijah said.

"Were you here the whole time we were speaking?" I asked.

"I was watching. We work together, so we are always close."

"I never thought of Enoch as a shepherd, or as one so full of joy. I am really looking forward to getting to know him better," I said.

"You have much to learn yet from both of us, but the joy you see in Enoch will not come from seeing Enoch, but from the way Enoch got it—walking with the Lord the way he did."

I wanted to ask Elijah another question, but was hesitating. He discerned this, and said, "Please ask what is on your heart."

"You walked with God too, and you were trusted with some of the greatest power He ever revealed through a prophet. Why aren't you as joyful as Enoch?" I inquired.

"I do not mind you asking, and this is important for you to understand. What you become in your life on earth will be who you are forever, without the carnality of course. If anyone on earth realized how much their life on earth impacted their eternity they would be in pursuit of the fruit of the Spirit more than any earthly treasure or accomplishment.

"The greatest treasure in all of creation is love. Love is the foundation of true joy and peace, and is the essence of what man was created to be. God is love, and if you walk with Him as you are called to, this will be your portion.

"I walked the earth during difficult and dark times. I walked with God and loved Him, but I let the evil of man overshadow the love I should have been growing in, for both God and people. I even delighted in calling fire down on people. It was necessary, but it was not necessary for me to enjoy it. I should have been weeping for them.

"Jonah had the greatest preaching gift until the Baptist. I was trusted with the greatest power since Moses. Neither Jonah nor I pursued love the way we should have, the way all should pursue it. If I had loved people more, even the ones I had to confront and bring judgment upon, many of them would not have perished, but would have been turned to the Lord instead.

"Without love, I became self-centered, and that is what cost me so that I was not able to finish my commission. Elisha had to finish what I had been called to do. One of the greatest mistakes a prophet can make is to not pursue loving God and loving others more than anything else."

After a short pause, as if to be sure I was grasping the importance of what he was saying, Elijah continued, "Those who are known as the great ones on the earth are not always well-known in heaven. Those who are known as the great ones in heaven are those who love the most.

"The evil that Enoch saw in his times was as bad, and in some ways worse, than the evil in my times. He kept his focus on loving God and walking with Him. Because of this, to some of the most evil and perverted souls, he prophesied hope and vision. He prophesied the coming of the Day of the Lord, and the glorious new beginning for the whole earth. He was a man of joy and a man of hope.

"To be a prophet in these times you must do some of the things that I did. You must confront the wicked and bring judgment upon them. You must confront the false teachers and false prophets. You must confront the evil leaders and authorities.

"To do this as you are called to do it, you must become more like Enoch than me. The judgments of God are His discipline for those whom He loves, and even His judgments that require destruction are done in love, not in retaliation. He never rejoices in destruction, but it is required at times to preserve others.

"Both Enoch and I are models of the prophets that will come forth in these times, but we are that model together. If you grow in love the way Enoch did, by walking with God, you will manifest the joy and peace of the Lord that will turn many from their wickedness; there will not need to be as much destruction."

"I do not mean to be disrespectful, but as I have read of your life many times, I have wondered if some of the things you did could have been done differently, and maybe the outcome would have been different," I said.

"Seeing the truth is never disrespectful. The Bible is the account of God's dealings with men, and men's dealings with God and one another. No one has yet served God perfectly but One. When we obey God it is required that we obey Him in His Spirit. If you obey Him in a wrong spirit the fruit can be very different than what He intended. I did do some things well, but I did not do everything He gave me to do in the right spirit. If I had walked in more love for God and love for His people things would have been different for many.

"Enoch was shown the great messengers of power that will come in the last days. I wasn't. He was given the honor of prophesying them because in character they will be more like him than me, but they will do all that I did and much more."

With that, Elijah walked off in the same direction as Enoch. I had almost too much to process. As I looked at the staff, I felt a connection to Enoch. I wanted to love people and release them into the joy of the Lord that he had. I was also sobered by Elijah's statement that we were now forming the character that we would have for eternity. This gave far more significance to every day. I did not ever want to miss another opportunity to grow in the fruit of the Spirit.

I thought about what scripture says that we should *'count it all joy when we encountered trials because the testing of our faith was more valuable than gold'*. "It is much more valuable," I thought. "How could any earthly treasure or accomplishment compare to something that would last forever?"

As I walked back to the camp, I prayed and beseeched the Lord to help me remember how crucial this is and for the anointing to convey it to others. I desperately wanted them all to meet Enoch and experience what I had.

As I got close enough to see the little group, I thought about how just a few minutes before I had been very close to despair. I was in despair because I considered myself a poor leader, thinking I had led those in my care away from the streams of living water. Now I felt that the whole wilderness journey was wonderful beyond description, and I really could be a shepherd to those I helped through it.

When I walked into the camp everyone was awake, alert, and they were all laughing.

"What is up?" I asked.

"The watchmen found water," William replied. "It was right under our feet. This one, James, said he felt we were on the right path, so the water had to be near; and if it was not above ground, then it had to be just below us. He started to dig and did not have to dig deep at all before it bubbled up."

"James, now that is the kind of discernment and wisdom we need in our watchman," I said to him, while stooping down to drink from the little stream now flowing through the middle of the camp.

"Where were you?" Mary asked.

"I had a meeting," I answered, noticing that Mark was looking at me intently.

"What are you thinking, Mark?" I inquired.

"I was told last night that you would have a message for us today that would guide us for the rest of our lives. I can also see that you have been given a shepherd's staff. Can you tell us now what the message is?" Mark replied.

"I can. I do have something to tell you that can help guide you the rest of your life," I began.

## CHAPTER FOURTEEN

# THE PROPHET

I was still so impacted by my meeting with Enoch that it took me a moment to gather myself before I could speak. I knew that what I had to say could guide them for the rest of their lives. I felt like I was about to show them the greatest treasure that had ever been found, and I wanted it to be as dramatic as possible to make the greatest possible impact.

I did not need drama, beating drums, or trumpets. Mark had already told them that I would return with a message that could guide them for the rest of their lives, and they were as focused as I had ever seen them. Even so, being with Enoch had done something to me, and the group could see it. This caused them to be even more attentive.

"We have made it this far without solid food. Even with the living water, we did get weaker after a few days, and last night we were near exhaustion. Today, we begin to draw on the solid food that will not only sustain us, but make us stronger every day. Our food is to do the Father's will, and the joy of the Lord will be our strength. New joy will be our companion, and we will grow in this every day that we stay on the path," I responded.

"But is there any real food that we will be given?" the older Mary asked.

"It is more real than any food you have ever had," I said. "The manna that sustained Israel was a type of this food. It is fresh bread from heaven that we will receive every day from now on."

"So, it is spiritual bread," Mary said, mocking good-naturedly.

"Is that not better than anything else we could eat?" I replied.

"It sounds good to me!" someone declared, to the happy agreement of everyone else. I was amazed by how good everyone seemed to be feeling.

"Now tell us about your meeting," Mary demanded, unable to contain her excitement and smiling like I had not seen before, "and tell us more about this message of the joy of the Lord."

"It's obvious that you have already found the joy of the Lord today," I started. "I just met the happiest person I have ever met. I just met with Enoch."

"What did he look like?" Mary interjected, still not able to contain herself. This irritated me a little, and I could not believe how quickly I could lose the good feeling I had after being with Enoch. I stopped, resolved not to be impatient, and continued.

"He looked like joy personified," I replied.

"But I thought he was a prophet?" someone remarked. "I don't think I've ever seen a prophetic person with much joy."

"Then you must not have ever seen a mature prophet," I responded. "Enoch was the first one about whom it was said that he prophesied, and he is the father of the prophets. If you are called to this ministry today and you mature as you should, you will be more like Enoch, and you will be one of the happiest people on earth.

"Enoch is a prophecy, a message from God. It is the most important message of all—we have been called to walk with God. That is the message that will keep us on the path of life. In His presence is the fullness of joy, and the joy that comes from being with Him is a food that gives us greater strength than any other food ever could."

"Enoch gave you the shepherd's staff, didn't he?" Mark asked.

"Yes, he did," I answered.

"It was cut from the tree. Did he tell you about the tree?" Mark continued.

"Yes, he did, but what do you know about the tree?" I asked Mark.

"I have seen the tree and the shepherd's staff. It's the Tree of Life. The authority of the shepherd comes from the Tree of Life. It is the fruit of that tree that you are to lead God's people to. It is the 'root of Jesse' that brought forth Christ who is our life. He is the food that is our joy, and His joy is our strength.

"It is also the rod of Aaron that sprouted. His rod sprouted because the staff of the shepherds is from the Tree of Life and is living. It is this life that helps us recognize the ones who have been sent by God and are the true shepherds," Mark said, pausing, but obviously able to continue.

"Mark, where did you get all of this understanding?" I asked.

"When I was given my calling as a prophet I was told that one of my assignments was to recognize those who had the shepherd's staff and to support them. I have only seen them in visions before, but I recognized that staff right away."

"Tell me all you know about it," I implored.

"You think your rod is new and freshly cut, but it is much older than you can imagine. It seems like it is new and fresh because of the life that is in it, and life will stay in it as long as you walk with God and do not depart from His path. This was cut from the Tree of Life before the world was formed, and it was sized just for you at that time. This is true of every shepherd's staff given to the shepherds, even those who lead the smallest company of God's people.

"Do you know why Enoch was the one who gave this to you?" Mark then asked.

"I know a little, but I think you may know more. Please tell me what you know."

"Enoch represents the path on which all true shepherds will lead God's people. True shepherds are known by their walk with God. They may be great counselors, healers, and teachers, but the shepherds will be known most of all by their walk with God and their closeness to Him. There are many things that can cause people to follow you, but the shepherds will be known by how they follow God on the path of life.

"One thing by which we can recognize shepherds that have stayed on the path of life is by their increasing joy. This was the joy you saw in Enoch. Shepherds who have stayed on the path of life do not seem to have cares or burdens because they are yoked with the One whose yoke is easy. These are not stressed, but are constantly energized by the strength that comes from the joy of the Lord. Their rod, or their authority, will be recognized by the life that is in them. Their rod will always be budding, bringing forth new life, because it comes from the Tree of Life Himself."

As Mark talked, everyone was enthralled, but some more so than others. I knew these were the shepherds. Deep was calling to deep, and their hearts were being awakened. As I watched Mark I could tell that he was also noting those who were being especially touched so that he could speak to them more at a later time. "What a gift he is to us," I thought, "and so young!"

"I am young, but I have already walked with God for a few years," Mark said, as if hearing my thoughts. Then he continued:

"Some claim to be able to use a 'diviner's rod' to find water under the ground; they are the counterfeits to what you have in your hand. Your rod can find the living waters that are hidden below the surface. Deep calls to deep, and life calls to life. Those who have the shepherd's rod become increasingly sensitive to what is life and where the waters of life are flowing," Mark said, and then hesitated as if he had more, but did not know if he should share it.

"Please continue," I said to him.

"When your rod buds you must gently break the buds off. Then you must give them to those who are being awakened to their calling as shepherds. These buds will grow with them, and each one will become a staff like yours," he said, again hesitating.

"Mark, please share all you know," I said.

"Okay. Those who receive the buds now and grow up to be shepherds at the end of the age will walk in the authority of the Shepherd. Their rod will be His rod in the earth. They will not just lead God's people and protect them from the enemy with the rod, but they will strike the enemies of the Lord. They will not just part seas, but they will part nations. They will lead God's people to the Promised Land."

"Why were you hesitant to share that, Mark?" I asked.

"Can I tell you privately?" he responded.

"If you think you need to, sure," I answered, and we walked a short distance from the rest.

"Your rod was a bud that was given to you when you were very young in the Lord," Mark began. "You did not carry it for long before you laid it down. In a sense, you did what Moses did when he threw his rod down at the Burning Bush. He was being commissioned as God's shepherd for His people, but did not feel adequate. When he threw the rod down it became a serpent and chased him until he picked it back up. That is what happens when you cast off the calling of the Lord."

"I know when I did that," I replied. "You are correct. Please continue."

"Like Moses, your rod became a serpent and chased you until you picked it up again, which was to take up your commission again," he continued.

"That is accurate," I responded, "and a good way to put it. When running from my calling all that I did prospered, but I was miserable. I felt that what I had dropped—my calling to ministry—was pursuing me day and night. You are right. Please continue."

"When you picked up the rod again and returned to your calling, it was like you had never missed a step in some ways, but stepped into a place much higher than you left. It was as if you had walked in your calling the whole time and grown into it," he said looking at me as I nodded that this was true.

"But you did miss something. You grew, and your rod grew, but for a long time it did not grow in your hand. Because of this you missed a lot. If you had grown together with your rod you would be more mature and more stable in your authority. You would be so one with the staff that it would be as another arm to your body. Now it is almost like something you are trying to get used to. You don't even know how to hold it right. Because of this you will be in danger of misusing this rod the same way Moses did."

"What you're saying is that I will be in danger of leading God's people to their Promised Land, but not be able to lead them into it?" I asked.

"That is the danger," Mark continued. "It is the danger for all who do not grow up together with their authority as they should."

"Mark, thank you for this warning. Is there anything else you have to say to me about this?" I asked.

"The Lord's grace is made perfect in weakness," Mark began. "You have a weakness because of the time you walked apart from your calling. This is the time when the enemy found access to you and your family that led to some of the greatest failures of your life, which are the failures with your family. Even though you see the results of your failures now, you have the promise of the Lord for your children and their children. They will serve the Lord and glorify His name. He who is faithful will bring this to pass.

"Your failures will not continue to be a liability if you lean on the Lord more because of your weakness, but you do have weaknesses. You must not cast down this rod again, and you must lean on Him constantly."

Again Mark hesitated for a minute as if to let that sink in, and then continued, "Even the least of the shepherds that are raised up from this place will be like David. They will be mighty warriors, mighty worshipers, and they will be great prophets like David.

"They must also have the joy of Enoch. Everyone in these times is going to need the joy of Enoch. Your remorse at your failures must be turned to joy because of the Redeemer who will redeem your mistakes."

I needed to hear what Mark shared with me as much as I needed to hear what Enoch and Elijah had shared with me. As much as I longed for more time with Enoch and Elijah, I did not want to miss what the Lord would say to me through those in our company. They could be just as much a messenger of the Lord as Enoch or Elijah.

I looked back at our little group. Everyone I had gotten to know really was a treasure, and more than remarkable. "The Lord has again saved His best for last," I thought. Again, Mark seemed to know what I was thinking.

"Some of the greatest to ever walk with God are either on this path or soon will be. The best part is not just getting to know Elijah and Enoch, but we will know the God of Elijah, the God of Enoch, the God of David, the God of Moses—the same God all of the great ones who walked this earth knew and served. Who could have even dreamed of a life like this?" Mark said echoing my thoughts.

"Who could have ever dreamed of something like this?" I agreed.

I did not wake up. I was not asleep. But you must wake up. You are being called to the mountain of the Lord.

NOW FEATURING WORK EDUCATIONAL PROGRAM
MorningStar University
School of Theology and Doctrine
School of the Holy Spirit
School of Missions
Releasing a Supernatural Army to Transform the World
BUILD Strong Biblical Foundations and a Christian Worldview
GAIN Practical and Supernatural Tools for Success
ENGAGE in "Special Forces" Mission Opportunities
INTERN with International Ministry, Education, and Business Leaders
1, 2, and 3 Year Programs Available
* Associate Degrees Available
NOW ACCEPTING APPLICATIONS
KNOW THE LORD
IMPACT HISTORY
CHANGE THE WORLD
FOR MORE INFORMATION
CALL: 803-802-5544, Extension 238
VISIT: www.MorningStarUniversity.com
EMAIL: MSUOffice@MorningStarMinistries.org

# BECOME A
# MORNINGSTAR
# PARTNER

**TRAIN**

**PROVIDE**

**RESTORE**

**EQUIP**

Our MorningStar Partners have grown into an extraordinary fellowship of men and women who are committed to seeing The Great Commission fulfilled in our times. Be a partner in the fruit of over 500 missionaries in the field and the raising up of a new breed of high-impact leadership who are advancing the faith around the globe, as well as building schools and orphanages. We are committed to multiplying the impact of the resources entrusted to us. Your monthly contribution of $20, $50, or $100 will make a difference!

In His Service,

## PARTNER WITH US TODAY

CALL: 800-542-0278
WEB: www.MorningStarMinistries.org
WRITE: Partners 375 Star Light Dr.
Fort Mill, SC 29715